Ready for Fall?

Near-Term Effects of Voluntary Summer
Learning Programs on Low-Income Students'
Learning Opportunities and Outcomes

Jennifer Sloan McCombs, John F. Pane, Catherine H. Augustine,
Heather L. Schwartz, Paco Martorell, and Laura Zakaras

Commissioned by

The Wallace Foundation

Supporting ideas.
Sharing solutions.
Expanding opportunities.

For more information on this publication, visit www.rand.org/t/rr815

Library of Congress Cataloging-in-Publication Data is available for this publication.

ISBN: 978-0-8330-8817-8

Published by the RAND Corporation, Santa Monica, Calif.

© Copyright 2014 RAND Corporation

RAND® is a registered trademark.

Cover design by Dori Gordon Walker

*Front cover, clockwise from top left: Vikram Raghuvanshi/iStock; TongRo Images/Thinkstock;
Digital Vision/Thinkstock; TongRo Images/Thinkstock; Digital Vision/Thinkstock*

Back cover: Monkey Business Images/Thinkstock

Support RAND

Make a tax-deductible charitable contribution at
www.rand.org/giving/contribute

www.rand.org

Preface

A typical student returns to school in the fall having lost some knowledge and skills gained in the previous school year. Prior research has determined that low-income students lose more ground over the summer than their higher-income peers. Prior research has also shown that some summer learning programs can stem this loss, but we know very little about whether large, district-run, voluntary programs can improve student outcomes.

To fill this gap, The Wallace Foundation launched the National Summer Learning Study in 2011. This five-year study offers the first-ever assessment of the effectiveness of large-scale, voluntary, district-run, summer learning programs serving low-income elementary students. The study, conducted by the RAND Corporation, uses a randomized controlled trial to assess the effects of district-run voluntary summer programs on student achievement and social and emotional skills over the short and long run. All students in the study were in the third grade as of spring 2013 and enrolled in a public school in one of five urban districts: Boston; Dallas; Duval County, Florida; Pittsburgh; or Rochester, New York.

The study follows these students from third to fifth grade. Our primary focus is on academic outcomes, but we also examine students' social-emotional outcomes as well as behavior and attendance during the school year. We have collected extensive data about the summer programs and instruction to help us examine how implementation is related to program effects.

This report is the second of five that will result from the study. The first report, *Getting to Work on Summer Learning: Recommended Practices for Success* (Augustine et al., 2013), offered lessons learned from detailed formative evaluations of the district programs in summer 2011. These evaluations, shared with districts in fall 2011, were designed to help the school districts improve the programs they offered in 2012. RAND completed another set of evaluations of the summer 2012 programs so that the districts could further strengthen their programs by summer 2013, when we launched a randomized controlled trial to assess effects on student performance. This report looks at how students in this study performed on mathematics, reading, and social-emotional assessments in fall 2013.

This study was undertaken by RAND Education, a unit of the RAND Corporation that conducts research on pre-K, K–12, and higher education issues such as preschool quality rating systems, assessment and accountability, teacher and leader effectiveness, school improvement, out-of-school time, educational technology, and higher education cost and completion.

This study was sponsored by The Wallace Foundation, which seeks to support and share effective ideas and practices to foster improvements in learning and enrichment for disadvantaged children and the vitality of the arts for everyone. Its current objectives are to improve the quality of schools, primarily by developing and placing effective principals in high-need schools; improve the quality of and access to afterschool programs through coordinated city systems and by strengthening the financial management skills of providers; reimagine and expand learning time during the traditional school day and year, as well as during the summer months; expand access to arts learning; and develop audiences for the arts. For more information and research on these and other related topics, please visit the Foundation's Knowledge Center at www.wallacefoundation.org.

Contents

Figures and Tables

Summary

Many students lose knowledge and skills over the summer. Summer learning loss disproportionately affects low-income students and therefore likely contributes to the achievement gap between these students and their higher-income peers. Until now, however, research has not demonstrated whether voluntary, school district-run summer learning programs offered to large numbers of urban, low-income students can improve student outcomes.

We assessed the effects of offering voluntary summer learning programs that include academic and enrichment activities to 3,194 elementary students in five districts across the country. (Another 2,445 students were assigned to a control group.) All students had completed third grade immediately before the summer program began; our assessments were based on data collected in the autumn after the programs ended.

This report is the second of five volumes from a five-year study, funded by The Wallace Foundation and conducted by the RAND Corporation, designed as a randomized controlled trial that assesses student outcomes in three waves: in the fall after the 2013 summer program (reported here), at the end of the school year following the program, and after a second summer program in 2014 (to show the cumulative effects of two summer programs). The goal of the study is to answer one key question: Do voluntary, district-run summer programs that include academics and enrichment activities improve student academic achievement and other outcomes, such as social and emotional competence?

This study is an evaluation of the effectiveness of low-income students' participation in summer learning programs in urban school districts. The five districts participating in the trial are Boston Public Schools, The Dallas Independent School District, Duval County Public Schools (Florida), Pittsburgh Public Schools, and The Rochester City School District (New York). The study required students who applied to be in the programs in the summer before they entered fourth grade to be randomized into the treatment group (that is, those accepted into the program) and the control group (those who did not get into the program) and hold that randomization status for two summers (summers 2013 and 2014). All the summer program leaders agreed to a set of common research-based elements:

- voluntary, full-day programming combining academics and enrichment for five days per week for no less than five weeks of the summer
- at least three hours of instruction (language arts and mathematics) per day taught by certified teachers
- small class sizes of no more than 15 students per class
- no fee to families for participation
- free transportation and meals.

Districts could also make many of their own choices about the design of their programs, such as how to manage their program sites, which enrichment activities to offer, the timing of the program during the summer, and the specific math and language arts curriculum (within some parameters, such as having one standardized curriculum across all sites within the district).

The study also provided districts with formative evaluations of their program implementation over two summers to drive program improvement before the randomized controlled trial began in summer 2013. This process was intended to ensure that districts, by applying best practices, were achieving certain quality standards before researchers evaluated the programs' effects on students.

This report informs practitioners and policymakers of the near-term effectiveness of summer learning programs, offered in urban districts to low-income students, each containing important, research-based common features. Because we evaluate five programs in five different contexts, each varying in terms of some key programmatic features such as specific curriculum, results from this study should be particularly compelling. We examine a "proof of concept" rather than the effectiveness of a particular program in a specific locale.

Early Results of Program Outcomes

Programs Served Community Needs

We found there was strong demand among low-income students and their families for free, voluntary programs that combine academics and enrichment. In addition, these district-run programs provided many students with opportunities for instruction and enrichment that they would not otherwise have had during the summer. Almost 60 percent of students in the control group, all of whom had applied to the districts' voluntary summer program but were denied admission, reported *not* attending any kind of summer program or camp over the summer.

Programs Improved Students' Mathematics Achievement

The programs had a significant positive effect on students' mathematics achievement when compared to students in the control group. The average effect size across the five school districts was 0.11.[1] This number reflects the spread in scores between the treatment group and the control group, and not the growth in learning from the beginning of the summer to the end in either group. The comparative difference in math performance is reasonably large for a five-week program. To put it in context, the average growth in student mathematics achievement between the spring of third grade and the spring of fourth grade is about a 0.52 effect size (Lipsey et al., 2012). Thus, treatment students began the 2013–2014 academic year with an advantage over their control group counterparts that appears meaningful relative to typical annual growth. A later phase of this study will explore whether teachers and students are able to capitalize on and sustain this advantage.

Programs Did Not Make a Difference in Reading Achievement

We found no differences between the treatment and control group students in reading skills. The difference was just 2 percent of a standard deviation and was not statistically significant. This finding is somewhat surprising because our study consists of primarily low-income students who, according to the research, lose more ground than other students in reading skills over the summer. Potential reasons for finding no effect in reading include the difficulty of improving reading comprehension skills, measurement issues, insufficient program length or hours of instruction, and insufficient instructional quality.

Programs Did Not Make a Difference in Students' Social-Emotional Competencies

Students in the program did no better on social-emotional outcomes than students in the control group. Our social-emotional measure includes items on self-regulation and self-motivation. While some district leaders thought their programs would have a positive effect in this area, only one program took specific action to focus on it by offering academic and enrichment staff professional development on instilling social and emotional competencies. The effect estimate in this district is positive and larger than the other districts, although not statistically significant.

Several Factors Correlated with Strong Outcomes

We also examined what aspects of the summer programs related to student outcomes: that is, whether factors such as high-quality instruction, instructional time, and site orderliness were correlated with better student outcomes. Unlike the randomized controlled trial, this part of our study is not experimental and therefore does not provide

---

[1] An effect size quantifies the difference between two groups. We report in standardized units, which enable comparisons across other studies and take into account the standard deviation (or spread) of scores of the sample.

definitive evidence of causal relationships. Still, it may lead to useful insights for district leaders who are committed to launching such programs or improving the ones they have. Out of seven program characteristics we analyzed, five were significantly correlated with improved learning in mathematics or reading for students in the treatment group.

- For mathematics (but not reading), strong attendance and more hours of academic instruction were linked to better outcomes. Students had a greater advantage in mathematics when they attended at least 22 days and received at least 13 hours of mathematics instruction. Effects were even larger for students who received 26 hours of instruction or more. These findings suggest that in order to maximize benefits for students, district should plan for programs that run five to six weeks and schedule 60–90 minutes of mathematics per day. Because student absences and inefficient use of time inside the day reduce instructional time on task, districts should make special efforts to promote consistent attendance, adhere to daily schedules, and ensure that teachers maximize instructional time inside the classroom.
- For reading (but not mathematics), instructional quality, teacher grade-level experience, and site orderliness were associated with better outcomes. These findings imply that districts should take particular care in trying to find the highest-quality reading teachers and those with experience in either the sending or receiving grade. Also, establishing clear expectations for student behavior, ensuring consistent application across teachers, and developing methods of maintaining positive student behavior in class may pay off in terms of student achievement in reading.

Next Steps

The next report we publish (in 2015) will describe the effect of one summer of programming on student achievement, attendance and behavior during the following school year. In our subsequent two reports (in 2016), we will assess the impact of two consecutive years of voluntary summer programming for urban students and the cost of this programming (see Figure S.1). This set of findings will build the knowledge base over time about how to design and implement summer learning programs, what outcomes they are likely to produce, and what practices are associated with success.

Figure S.1
Schedule of Summer Learning Demonstration Public Reports

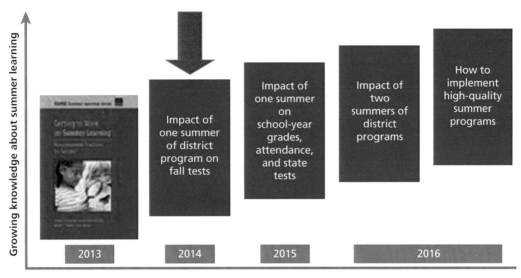

Acknowledgments

Many people helped in conducting this study and producing this report. We would like to thank those at The Wallace Foundation for their substantive and financial support. Ann Stone, Elizabeth Ty Wilde, and Edward Pauly provided valuable guidance on the intellectual and analytic components of our work. Lucas Held and Daniel Browne provided greatly appreciated feedback on this report.

Representatives from the Boston, Dallas, Duval County, Pittsburgh, and Rochester summer programs generously allowed us access to observe their programs and time to interview and survey stakeholders. We are particularly grateful to the people who allowed us to interview or observe them and to those who completed the surveys. Program materials and district data were provided when requested and we appreciate the time that goes into fulfilling those requests.

Several RAND staff members contributed to the data analyses and therefore to this report. Scott Naftel received, cleaned, and prepared all of the data we received from the districts. Courtney Kase, Terry Marsh, Andrea Phillips, and Susannah Faxon-Mills observed instruction and collected survey data in the five districts.

Our reviewers Laura Hamilton, J.R. Lockwood, and James Kim improved the document itself. Finally, Arwen Bicknell provided excellent editing services. We acknowledge their help in improving this document.

Abbreviations

ARC	American Reading Company
BPS	Boston Public Schools
CBO	community-based organization
DESSA	Devereux Student Strengths Assessment
DESSA-RRE	DESSA RAND Research Edition
FRPL	free or reduced-price lunch
GMADE	Group Mathematics Assessment and Diagnostic Evaluation
GRADE	Group Reading Assessment and Diagnostic Evaluation
IEP	individualized education plan
ITT	intent-to-treat
SDA	Summer Dreamers Academy
SLP	Summer Learning Project
TOT	treatment effect on the treated

CHAPTER ONE

Introduction

The United States has a persistent achievement gap between students from low-income and higher-income families. On the 2013 National Assessment of Educational Progress, 47 percent of fourth-grade students eligible for free or reduced-price lunch (FRPL) scored at the "below basic" level in reading compared with 17 percent of students who were not eligible—a gap of 30 percentage points. For mathematics, the gap was 20 percentage points (27 percent versus 7 percent). Similar, although smaller, achievement gaps are found between black and white students, Hispanic and white students, and English language learners and native speakers. These income, racial, and language-learner achievement gaps persist into later grades (Reardon, 2011; U.S. Department of Education, 2014).

The achievement gap is due in part to inequities in opportunities and experiences during children's earliest years that persist outside the school day during children's K–12 years. For this reason, policymakers are increasingly looking toward interventions outside the traditional school day, such as early childhood education and after-school and summer programming, to help supplement school efforts to close these gaps in achievement. Research demonstrates that students lose knowledge and skills over summer breaks, particularly low-income students who face greater losses in reading than higher-income peers (Cooper, Nye, et al., 1996). In addition to holding promise for closing achievement gaps, summer programs can also benefit struggling students who need additional time to master grade-level content.

Research on Summer Learning Programs

Because "summer slide" in academic achievement is common, especially for low-income students in reading, a number of school districts and youth development organizations have offered structured programs of summer instruction to counteract the slide. While prior research provides evidence regarding mandatory district-run programs and small, voluntary programs operated outside of districts, until now there has been no research evidence regarding the effectiveness of voluntary, district-run summer learning programs offered to large numbers of students. Consequently, district leaders do not know whether the provision of summer learning opportunities for students who are not required to attend programs for grade recovery is a wise investment.

However, a body of research has documented that some, though not all, small summer programs, reading-at-home programs, and mandatory summer learning programs have been effective in improving student achievement. Meta-analyses have found positive effects of summer programming in reading (Cooper, Charlton, et al., 2000; Kim and Quinn, 2013) and mathematics (Cooper, Charlton, et al., 2000). In rigorous observational and experimental studies,[1] positive effects on student achievement have been documented for school district–run mandatory summer programs (Jacob and Lefgren, 2004; Matsudaira, 2008; and McCombs, Kirby, and Mariano, 2009), as well as for small, voluntary summer programs not run by school districts (Borman, Benson, and Overman, 2005; Schacter and Jo, 2005; Chaplin and Capizzano, 2006; and Borman, Goetz, and Dowling, 2009), and non-classroom–based, reading-at-home programs (James Kim, 2006; Kim and White, 2008; and Allington et al., 2010).

However, other studies have found no overall effects for reading in small, voluntary summer programs (Borman, Goetz, and Dowling, 2009) or reading-at-home programs (Jimmy Kim, 2004; Kim and Guryan, 2010; Wilkins et al., 2012; and White et al., 2013). Another study found no evidence that attending a summer program after completing the fifth grade improved students' mathematics scores in sixth grade (Mariano and Martorell, 2013).[2]

In these studies, the primary goal of the summer programs was to improve academic outcomes. However, some summer program leaders also espouse a desire to improve students' nonacademic outcomes through these programs (Augustine et al., 2013). In earlier work (McCombs et al., 2011), we hypothesized that nonacademic outcomes may result indirectly from improved academic achievement due to the program (e.g., students who perform better in school feel more confident and have improved behavior). It is also possible that a summer learning program that is structured to intentionally affect students' social-emotional outcomes may do so. An evaluation of Building Educated Leaders for Life (BELL) examined whether that program influenced nonacademic outcomes. Authors found it affected the degree to which parents encouraged their children to read but it did not influence students' academic self-perceptions or social behaviors (Chaplin and Capizzano, 2006).

---

[1]   In observational studies, researchers do not control the assignment of students to treatment status. A weakness in such studies is that the two groups may differ in unmeasured ways that may bias treatment effect estimates. In experimental studies, students are randomly selected to either receive the treatment or serve in a control group, helping to ensure the two groups are identical.

[2]   This is a reanalysis of the New York City grade retention summer program findings documented in McCombs et al., 2009, in which the authors concluded that, for students who scored just below failing, there was no evidence that attending the fifth-grade summer program generated improvements in sixth-grade mathematics achievement. These findings are not generalizable to students who are far below grade-level expectations.

Research Questions

After a review of existing research on summer loss and summer programs, and after gathering information on the challenges that districts face in developing and sustaining voluntary summer programs (documented in McCombs et al., 2011), The Wallace Foundation launched the National Summer Learning Study in 2011. This five-year study provides the first-ever assessment of the effectiveness of large-scale, voluntary, district-run summer learning programs serving low-income elementary students. It examines effectiveness using a randomized controlled trial study design. One of the major challenges of social science research is to measure the counterfactual—i.e., what would have happened to students if they did not receive the intervention. A randomized controlled trial creates this counterfactual. In this study design, researchers randomly assign students who are participating in the study into two groups—one that receives the intervention and one that does not. This process assures that any differences between the outcomes of the students in the two groups can be attributed to the program being evaluated rather than some other factor.

Over the course of the five-year study, the RAND Corporation will answer the following research questions:

1. What is the effect of school district–run voluntary summer programs that combine academic and enrichment activities on low-income students' reading and math outcomes?
2. Do student characteristics, such as achievement level, race/ethnicity, family income, or English-language learner status, influence those outcomes?
3. What program implementation factors relate to student outcomes? To what extent is student attendance related to student outcomes?
4. What is the effect of these programs on students' social and emotion competence?
5. What is the effect of these programs on school year attendance, grades, and behavior?
6. What is the effect of two consecutive summers of voluntary summer programming on student achievement and other outcomes? What factors are related to these outcomes?
7. Do the effects of summer learning programs persist over time?
8. How can districts implement summer learning programs that include features that most benefit students?
9. Are these programs cost-effective?

This report examines research questions 1, 2, and 3 by examining near-term outcomes—those gathered in the fall soon after the first summer of programming ended. Questions 1 and 2 will be addressed again in the future using school year and spring assessment data.

Phases of the Study

Initiated in 2011, this study is scheduled to continue at least through 2016 and consists of three phases (Figure 1.1).

Phase I

Phase I took place between spring 2011 and fall 2012. The Wallace Foundation originally selected six districts—Boston, Cincinnati, Dallas, Duval County (Florida), Pittsburgh, and Rochester (New York)—to join the study in spring 2011. These districts, which already offered voluntary summer learning programs to their students, were willing to adopt certain common programming elements and participate in a randomized controlled trial. While districts were allowed to make many programmatic design choices that resulted in considerable variation within and across districts, all were required to enact a set of common elements:

1.   voluntary, full-day programming combining academics and enrichment for five days per week for no less than five weeks of the summer
2.   at least three hours of instruction (language arts and mathematics) per day provided by certified teachers
3.   small class sizes of no more than 15 students per class
4.   no fee to families for participation
5.   free transportation and meals.

To help the districts strengthen and expand their programs, The Wallace Foundation provided supplemental funding for program operations and supported improvement through curricular consultants, peer collaboration, and external formative evaluation. RAND conducted formative evaluations of program implementation in each district in summers 2011 and 2012, providing feedback and recommendations to the districts each fall.

Figure 1.1
Three Phases of the Project

The Foundation purposefully built in two years of formative evaluation and program strengthening prior to launching the randomized controlled trial. For some districts, the formative feedback led to program improvements year after year. But in one district, there was not steady improvement as leadership and staffing changes resulted in inconsistent implementation over time. Other districts faced other challenges that were not overcome—for instance, despite their efforts, program leaders in three districts were unable to improve attendance rates over time.

During this first phase, RAND also scanned each city's summer offerings to assess the level of "service contrast" between the district program and other summer programs offered in the community. Because the randomized controlled trial compares outcomes of treatment and control students to measure the program effect, it was important to understand what students in the control group experienced during the summer. If there was little contrast between the summer experiences of the treatment and control group, the study would end up examining the effectiveness of one voluntary summer program relative to another, which was not the intent. In Cincinnati, due in part to the superintendent's strong advocacy for summer learning in the community, we found a number of nondistrict summer programs that incorporated academics. In consultation with RAND, The Foundation determined that the level of service contrast between Cincinnati Public Schools' summer program and others within the city was insufficient to justify including the district in Phase II of the study.

Phases II and III

The second phase of the study, which began in spring 2013, is the randomized controlled trial,[3] an ambitious and rigorous experiment that randomly assigns students with similar characteristics into two groups: one that participates in the intervention and one that does not.

After districts recruited third-graders for the program in spring 2013, RAND randomized applicants into two groups in each of the five participating school districts. Students assigned to the treatment group were accepted into the program for both summer 2013 and 2014. Students assigned to the control group were not allowed to attend the program in either of those two summers. In each district, more students applied to the program than could be served with existing funds, which made randomization a reasonable method of determining which students could attend the programs.

---

[3] For the design and implementation of the experiment and analysis of the results, RAND formed a distinct, independent team of methodologists and analysts who were not engaged in the Phase I formative evaluations and were not involved in the ongoing collection of implementation data and formative feedback to districts. This strategy of independent teams was adopted to help ensure that the conduct of the experiment and analysis of the results would not be influenced by involvement in program improvement efforts.

RAND also studied implementation of the summer programs in 2013 and 2014 and continued to provide formative feedback to the districts to support program improvement.

In Phase III, RAND will track and analyze student outcomes at least through the end of the 2014–2015 school year, and perhaps beyond.

Schedule of Public Reports

Figure 1.2 illustrates the series of five reports that will result from the study. The first report provided strategies and steps to create an effective summer learning program gleaned from two years of formative program evaluation. This report, the second in the series, is the first to describe program effects on student outcomes. It is one piece of a larger set of evidence that will emerge over the next two years. This report focuses on how students performed on assessments administered in fall 2013, shortly after the first summer program. Our report in 2015 will provide readers with a more complete understanding of the effect of one summer of programming on student achievement, grades, attendance, and behavior during the following school year. A fourth report will assess the effectiveness of two years of voluntary summer programming. And finally, based on the full range of implementation and outcome findings, we will publish a fifth report focused

Figure 1.2
Schedule of Summer Learning Demonstration Public Reports

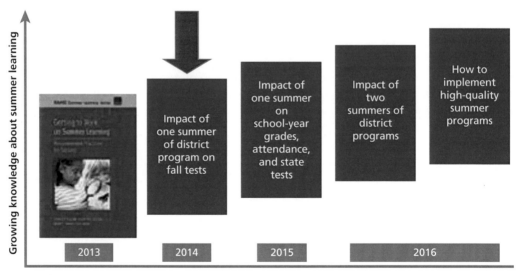

on research-based strategies for designing and implementing summer programs. The full set of findings from the five reports will establish a well-developed knowledge base about how to design and implement voluntary summer learning programming, what outcomes they are likely to produce, and what practices are associated with success.

Contribution of the Study

The study makes an important contribution to research and policy. It is the first study to rigorously test the effectiveness of large-scale, district-run voluntary programs that combine academics and enrichment. The programs share common core characteristics: at least three hours of instruction (language arts and mathematics) per day taught by certified teachers; small class sizes of no more than 15 students per class; and no fee to families for participation that includes transportation and meals. Districts could also make many of their own choices about the design of their programs, such as how to manage their program sites, which enrichment activities to offer, the timing of the program during the summer, and the specific math and language arts curriculum (within some parameters, such as having one standardized curriculum across all sites within the district). By evaluating programming in multiple settings, the study tests the effectiveness of these types of programs as they are actually implemented by several school districts throughout the country, rather than the effectiveness of a certain program in a specific setting. It also tests the impact of offering this program for two consecutive summers. And, in addition to examining academic achievement (the primary objective of our study), we also measure students' social-emotional outcomes, as well as their behavior and attendance during the school year. The study collects an extensive set of implementation measures, which enable us to investigate whether programmatic features, such as instructional quality and hours of instruction, are related to program effects. The study also tracks program costs, so we can determine cost effectiveness of the programs. By the end of 2016, policymakers and practitioners will have a greater understanding of the impacts of these programs, their costs, and the features that appear to be most important when considering low-income, urban students' performance.

Caveats

We note here three caveats to the results described in this report:

- We purposefully administered common, standardized general mathematics and reading tests approximately one month after the summer programs ended. The tests took one to one-and-a half hours to complete. Because they are general assessments of content, they may not capture the many and varied skills and topics that the districts chose to focus on during the summer. Future reports will also assess impacts on other student outcomes measures, such as grades, attendance, behavior, and state tests.

- We compared the fall 2013 scores on these tests of students who were admitted to the program to students who were not admitted, with statistical adjustment for students' performance in the previous school year. Thus, we can calculate whether the summer programs conferred an advantage to the treatment students relative to the control group students. Our study was not intended to measure summer slide, so students in the study did not take the same test both before and after summer 2013. As a result, the data cannot tell us whether they experienced summer slide, held steady, or advanced in their mathematics or reading skills during the summer.

- We recruited a sufficient number of students to detect a meaningful impact of the summer programs when student outcomes are combined across all of the programs. We did not design the study to detect impacts of the individual district programs.

Report Overview

The report is organized into seven chapters. In Chapter Two, we discuss how we measured program implementation and outcomes, describing all the sources of data we collected, including direct observations, surveys, district data, and academic and social-emotional assessments, and providing an overview of the methods we use to analyze outcomes. Chapter Three describes the students in the study, including the numbers enrolled in each district's program, their demographics, and their summer activities. Chapter Four briefly describes the programs and how they varied in implementation. In Chapter Five, we present the first results of the randomized controlled trial. Chapter Six describes the program characteristics that appear to contribute to improved outcomes. Finally, Chapter Seven recaps our key findings and their implications.

CHAPTER TWO

How Did We Measure Implementation and Outcomes?

The goal of the study is to assess the impact of summer learning programs on student outcomes. But we also assume that for the programs to have impact, they have to be implemented well—for example, providing quality instruction to students who attend consistently. Therefore we collected data on program implementation in each of the two summers of the experiment. To assess how the summer programs were implemented, we observed each student's math and language arts classroom at least once; surveyed academic teachers in the summer program; and tracked student attendance. To measure outcomes in fall 2013, The Foundation worked with the districts to make testing arrangements and contracted a firm to test study participants on both reading and mathematics in the first four weeks of school. We also asked homeroom teachers of treatment and control students to fill out a survey reporting on each student's social-emotional competencies about three months after the beginning of school. Each of these data collection efforts is briefly described below. Instruments and technical detail regarding scales and methods are presented in an online appendix to this report (McCombs, Pane, et al., 2014, Appendix C).

Program Implementation

The summer programs were delivered at 35 sites across the five school districts; the number of sites per district ranged from three to ten. Most of the sites were district-owned school buildings; a minority was partner-operated, such as at a nature preserve. In each site, certified district teachers taught mathematics and language arts. Most teachers were departmentalized, meaning that they taught only math or only language arts. These teachers typically taught two different groups of students each day for roughly an hour and a half each. Some teachers had self-contained classrooms in which they taught both subjects, typically to the same single group of students. There were approximately 230 certified academic teachers instructing the students in our study across the five districts. In the academic classrooms, average student class sizes ranged from eight to 14 students. In most of the sites, students participated in academics in the morning and enrichment in the afternoon, such as tennis, dance, theater, fencing, and rock climbing. These activities were sometimes offered at the same site where academic classes were offered; in other cases, students were bused to other facilities.

Because we assume that program outcomes are related to implementation, we collected extensive implementation data, as described later. We used multiple sources of data to assess dimensions of the program we expected would relate to outcomes. These included exposure to and quality of instruction, opportunities for social and emotional development in the classrooms, appropriateness of the curriculum, orderliness of the site, and qualification of the teachers. Attendance data and classroom observations provided information on dosage, instructional quality, and opportunities for social-emotional development. Teacher survey results provided information on their qualifications, as well as the appropriateness of the curriculum and the orderliness of the site.

Classroom Observation Ratings

We conducted classroom observations to estimate the number of instructional hours each student received, instructional quality, and opportunities for social-emotional development. We followed each summer homeroom class of students through an entire day of their program. This means a single observer observed each classroom in each of the summer programs at least once, which resulted in 748 observed classroom sessions in summer 2013. Table 2.1 lists the number of classrooms we observed by subject and district. Because we observed each class, we observed a teacher more than once if the teacher taught more than one subject or more than one group of students.

Instructional Hours

Because time spent on academic instruction was so critical to our assessments, observers noted classroom activities in a running time log and coded each time segment as instruc-

Table 2.1
Number of Classroom Observations

Subject Area	Boston	Dallas	Duval	Pittsburgh	Rochester	Total
Language Arts	57	56	46	16	36	211
Writing (additional)	—	—	—	—	24	24
Walk to Intervention (additional reading)	—	—	—	—	47	47
Enrichment	66	71	70	11	21	240
Mathematics	34	56	38	16	34	178
Science	—	—	26	—	—	26
Success Maker	—	—	22	—	—	22
Total	157	183	202	43	162	748

NOTE: Dashes indicate that the subject area was not taught in the district.

tional or noninstructional time. In addition to the required mathematics and reading classes, some districts provided additional classes that entered into the tallies of academic instruction. For example, in Rochester, students had an additional writing and an additional reading intervention class. For the latter, students were placed in groups based on an assessment of their reading skills. Within these small groups, teachers worked on reading strategies that were appropriate for their students' reading levels. In Duval, students went to a science class and a "Success Maker" class. In the latter, students used Success Maker, a computer-based learning tool that provides individual-level activities in reading and mathematics. To calculate the instructional hours each student received, we combined his or her days of attendance at the summer program with his or her classroom's instructional time over the summer in both language arts and mathematics.

Instructional Quality

We also rated each classroom on 34 indicators of instruction and interaction in the classroom. We used the classroom observation data to create an index of instructional quality. We calculated instructional quality at the individual student's language arts/mathematics classroom level. To do this, we summed the items in the scale that are listed in Table 2.2. These instructional quality ratings contain error due to the small number of observations of each individual classroom and disagreements among raters. Online Appendixes C and D describe measures we took to mitigate error from these sources.

Table 2.2
Measures of (Language Arts/Mathematics) Instructional Quality

Scale Items	Scale
The observed percentage of class time that was spent on instruction.	Ranges from 0 to 1 point
"The teacher exhibited obvious signs of enthusiasm about the content of the class."	1 point if yes
"Large majority of students are on-task throughout the class. Students are focused and attentive to the task/project."	1 point if yes
"The teacher provided or failed to correct factually inaccurate information that would confuse students about the content/skills they were to learn."	1 point if no
"The teacher explained the purpose of the class in terms of real-world relevance."	1 point if yes
"The teacher's explanation of the instructional content was unclear or hard to follow."	1 point if no
"The teacher: (1) performed ongoing assessment throughout the whole class period by checking for students' understanding of content, and (2) addressed misunderstandings if and as they arose."	1 point if yes
"When the teacher disciplined students, the majority of the class was interrupted for a long period."	1 point if no or not applicable
"The teacher responsible for the activity was disengaged in the classroom because of distractions by factors that were within her control."	1 point if no
"All or almost all students exhibited obvious signs of enthusiasm for the class throughout the class period (e.g., jumping out of seat, quickly and enthusiastically answering teacher's questions)."	1 point if yes

Teacher Survey

We administered a short survey to summer math and language arts teachers, and we used the results to create measures of site orderliness and appropriateness of the curriculum. The survey was customized for each district (for example, to allow teachers to identify the name of the summer site where they worked). An example of the teacher survey is included in online Appendix C. The survey took five to ten minutes to complete and was administered in the last two weeks of each district's summer program. Topics covered professional development, provision of student data to teachers, summer mathematics and reading curricula, climate and culture of the summer program, and student behavior. Table 2.3 shows the number of teachers who took the survey and response rates. We obtained very high response rates, and we are therefore confident that survey respondents were representative of academic teachers in the programs.

Appropriateness of the (Mathematics/Language Arts) Curriculum

We expected that if summer programs used a curriculum that teachers deemed appropriate for their students, then the effectiveness of summer programming in boosting student achievement would likely be enhanced. Appropriateness was defined on a scale that combined teacher perceptions about reasonable pacing, clarity of curriculum, whether the curriculum addressed the right gaps in student knowledge and skills, and whether it was fun for students (Table 2.4). This scale is derived from items on the academic teacher survey. It is a teacher-level construct and associated with the treatment students assigned to that mathematics/language arts teacher. In the survey, teachers who reported teaching mathematics during summer 2013 were prompted to answer mathematics curriculum questions, with a parallel structure for language arts teachers. Teachers who taught both subjects were asked to complete both sets of curriculum questions. The mathematics curriculum scale includes four items and the language arts curriculum scale includes five.

Table 2.3
Number of Respondents to Teacher Survey

	Boston	Dallas	Duval	Pittsburgh	Rochester	Total
Mathematics						
Total teachers (N)	30	33	27	8	17	115
Total respondents (N)	30	30	24	8	17	109
Response rate (%)	100	91	89	100	100	95
Language arts						
Total teachers (N)	30	36	27	8	22	123
Total respondents (N)	30	32	26	8	20	116
Response rate (%)	100	89	96	100	91	94

Table 2.4
Appropriateness of (Mathematics/Language Arts) Curriculum Scale Items

Scale Items
1–4 points on agreement on: The planned pacing of the curriculum was reasonable.
1–4 points on agreement on: The mathematics curriculum is clear for me to follow.
1–4 points on agreement on: The mathematics curriculum addresses gaps that many students have from last year.
1–4 points on agreement on: The mathematics curriculum includes fun, interesting activities for students.
1–4 points on agreement on: [for language arts only] The language arts curriculum provides students with texts that are appropriate for their reading level.

Site Discipline and Order

Like the social-emotional development scale, this is a site-level scale, but derived from teacher survey data within each site. Our working hypothesis was that sites that teachers deemed safe (free of bullying and fighting) and having a clear set of procedures for student discipline may have better attendance and allow more time to be spent on academic instruction, rather than on discipline. Items in the scale (listed in Table 2.5) were first summed within a teacher respondent and then averaged across respondents for a site-level scale score.

Attendance Data

We collected data from each district on students' daily attendance in the summer programs. To increase the accuracy of attendance data collected from districts' electronic records, we also collected supplemental data. For example, in one district, we collected hard-copy attendance records from each site, which we used to check and correct suspicious electronic attendance records (e.g., 100 percent attendance at a site on the last day of the program, which suggested that no attendance was electronically entered for that day).

Table 2.5
Site Discipline and Order Scale Items

Scale Items	Scale
"Children are bullied and harassed by other students at least once a week."	1–4 points on agreement
"Children get into physical fights with other students at school at least once a week."	1–4 points on agreement
"The procedure for handling student discipline problems is effective."	1–4 points on agreement
"There is a clear procedure for handling student discipline problems."	1–4 points on agreement
"Due to student misbehavior, a great deal of learning time is wasted."	1–4 points on disagreement

Student Outcomes

We next describe how we collected data on student outcomes. These data were collected for both the treatment and control group students in the study.

Academic Assessments

The primary outcome of interest for this near-term analysis was students' performance on standardized assessments of their generalized mathematics and reading achievement. We selected generalized mathematics and reading assessments, rather than curriculum-based assessments, to administer in the fall for two reasons. First, by design, not all of the programs implemented the same curriculum. Second, we assume that policymakers have a greater interest in how summer learning programs benefit students in terms of their general reading and mathematics knowledge and skills—skills that can be capitalized on during the subsequent school year, as opposed to student mastery of a specific curriculum.

The majority of students took the Group Mathematics Assessment and Diagnostic Evaluation (GMADE) mathematics assessment and Group Reading Assessment and Diagnostic Evaluation (GRADE) reading assessment by Pearson Education, which are 90-minute and 65-minute multiple-choice paper tests, respectively (Table 2.6). These assessments were selected after piloting them along with other generalized assessments in summer 2012. We did not find that the piloted tests were either too difficult or too easy for a majority of students. The Pearson products had implementation and cost advantages relative to the alternatives, which is why they were selected.

These exams are offered at various levels that roughly correspond to grade levels, but are designed with flexibility to administer the test above or below the grade level indicated. For example, Level 3 is nominally for third-graders, but is considered appropriate for second- or fourth-graders as well. Students in the study were all fourth-graders in fall 2013 (with rare exceptions of grade retention or advancement), following the summer program. We selected the Level 3 exam for the students in the study because they are generally low-performing students and because the tests would be administered very early in fourth grade.

Modified versions of this assessment plan were used in two districts. In Pittsburgh, the district was already administering the GRADE Level 4 assessment to all of its fourth-graders for a different initiative and we elected to make use of those existing test results. In Dallas, students who took the Texas spring 2013 assessment in Spanish rather than in English were administered the reading comprehension subtest of the Spanish-language Logramos from Riverside Publishing rather than the GRADE. Online Appendix C discusses how the scores from the various assessments were combined for analysis.

The Wallace Foundation contracted the research firm Mathematica Policy Research to administer these assessments to students in the study. The assessments were

Table 2.6
Fall 2013 Mathematics and Reading Assessments

District	Mathematics			Reading		
	Type of Assessment Administered	Number of Students with Scorable Tests	Response Rate (%)	Type of Assessment Administered	Number of Students with Scorable Tests	Response Rate (%)
Boston	Level 3 GMADE	870	91	Level 3 GRADE	874	91
Dallas	Level 3 GMADE	1,861	91	Level 3 GRADE For ELL, Logramos reading comprehension subtest	1,857 (889 GRADE & 968 Logramos)	90
Duval	Level 3 GMADE	817	92	Level 3 GRADE	812	91
Pittsburgh	Level 3 GMADE	587	90	Level 4 GRADE administered by district	565	86
Rochester	Level 3 GMADE	992	92	Level 3 GRADE	991	92
Total		5,127	91		5,099	90

NOTE: Unless otherwise noted, the assessments were administered to students by Mathematica Policy Research.

administered in fall 2013 within four weeks of the beginning of the school year. Only students in the study who were still enrolled in a public school within the five school districts were eligible for fall 2013 testing. Across all districts, the overall percentage of students in the study who moved out of the school district and those whose location was unknown at the time of testing was 7.4 percent. Pittsburgh had the highest percentage of unavailable students at 9.1 percent, followed by Dallas with 9.0 percent, and Duval with 7.5 percent. Boston and Rochester had the lowest percentage of students not available for testing at 5.5 percent and 4.8 percent, respectively. In total, we have mathematics scale scores for 5,127 students in the study (91 percent) and reading scale scores (either Logramos or GRADE) for 5,099 students in the study (90 percent). This is a very high testing rate, given that 7.4 percent of the study students attrited.

Student Survey

At the same time that Mathematica Policy Research administered tests in fall 2013, they also administered a four-question survey to students in both the treatment group and the control group about whether they participated in any type of summer program or camp. These data allowed us to distinguish between control group students who reported they participated in an academic summer learning program for at least a few weeks and control group students who reported no exposure to academic programming over the summer. Students who took the Spanish reading test took a Spanish version of this survey.

Devereux Student Strengths Assessment

Broadly, social-emotional competence refers to the ability of students to successfully interact with other students and adults in a way that demonstrates an awareness of, and ability to manage, emotions in an age- and context-appropriate manner. To measure social-emotional competencies, RAND administered a version of the Devereux Student Strengths Assessment (DESSA) (LeBuffe, Shapiro, and Naglieri, 2009) during the fall term to the homeroom teachers of students in the study. The DESSA was selected after reviewing 17 social-emotional outcomes measures. For all of these measures, we considered the ages of students assessed and the instruments' validity and reliability for those age groups. We also considered the burden on participants. The DESSA emerged as the top choice—although, based on a review of peer-reviewed journal literature, it has not been used to measure the impact of interventions in a school setting. It has been used primarily to measure growth in social-emotional competencies as a result of out-of-school interventions specifically designed to improve these outcomes (see, e.g., Pendrey and Roeter, 2013; Pendrey et al., 2014).

Working with the developers of the DESSA, RAND staff selected 27 items from the original item pool of 72 items, based on their alignment with the school districts' stated goals for their summer programming. Using student data from the DESSA national standardization sample, the developers determined that these items had a high degree of reliability. This version, the DESSA RAND Research Edition (DESSA-RRE), is shown in Table 2.7.[1]

Starting in the 11th week of the school year, homeroom teachers of students in the study were asked to complete the DESSA-RRE survey online. This timing was chosen to ensure that the large majority of students would have been assigned to their homeroom for at least four weeks. Each item of the survey asked the teacher to rate on a 5-point scale how often the student engaged in a particular behavior over the past

Table 2.7
DESSA-RRE Social-Emotional Behavior Items

During the past 4 weeks, how often did the child... (Response options: Never, Rarely, Occasionally, Frequently, Very Frequently)
Carry herself/himself with confidence
Keep trying when unsuccessful
Say good things about herself/himself
Compliment or congratulate someone
Show good judgment
Pay attention
Wait for her/his turn
Act comfortable in a new situation
Do things independently
Respect another person's opinion
Contribute to group efforts
Do routine tasks or chores without being reminded
Perform the steps of a task in order
Show creativity in completing a task
Share with others
Accept another choice when his/her first choice was unavailable
Say good things about the future
Stay calm when faced with a challenge
Attract positive attention from adults
Cooperate with peers or siblings
Show care when doing a project or school work
Make a suggestion or request in a polite way
Learn from experience
Work hard on projects
Follow rules
Offer to help somebody
Adjust well when going from one setting to another

---

[1]   This table is repeated in Chapter Two of the online appendix, along with reliability statistics.

four weeks. Some of these teachers may have taught the students during the summer program, which would mean that they would have been aware of whether the student attended the program. However, none of the districts systematically informed fourth-grade teachers of which students had attended the summer program and which had not.

The survey took approximately five minutes to complete per student. Teachers, who received a $20 Amazon gift card for each survey completed, were required to answer at least 26 of the 27 items for a survey to be deemed complete. We obtained responses from 84 percent of homeroom teachers and for 79 percent of the study students. The effective response rate was 86 percent of the students still enrolled in the districts.[2]

Analytic Methods Used to Estimate Program Effects

To estimate the average effect of the summer programs on students, we used two methods. The first is called *intent-to-treat* (ITT) analysis. This approach compares outcomes for all treatment students against the outcomes of all control students, regardless of whether they ever attended the program (or whether the control students were accidentally allowed to participate in the program). In other words, it includes the no-shows and crossovers in outcome averages. It represents the average treatment effect of offering a summer learning program on all students who sign up for it. The ITT approach typically produces smaller effect sizes because students who were assigned to the treatment group but did not show up are included in average treatment group outcomes. Also, crossover students assigned to the control group who attended the treatment program by mistake are included in the control group outcomes, even though they likely benefited from the program. To address these limitations of the ITT analysis, we also conduct *treatment effect on the treated* (TOT) analysis. This approach estimates the effect of the program on those who attended the program for at least one day. It represents the average treatment effect that districts should expect for students who attend the program.

---

[2]   To estimate this response rate, we used district data on students who had left the district as of the time we administered the DESSA-RRE.

CHAPTER THREE

Who Were the Students in the Study?

This chapter describes characteristics of the students in the study, as well as attendance patterns for both the treatment and control students in summer programs. Differences between the two groups depend to some extent on the attendance rate of the treatment students and whether the control students sought out other summer opportunities when they were not accepted into the program.

Study Student Characteristics

In spring 2013, summer program leaders in each district set criteria for selecting the third-graders they would invite to the voluntary summer program. District criteria varied. One district advertised to and recruited all third-graders. The other four districts excluded students at risk of grade retention, targeting all other third-graders, except for one district that also excluded its highest-performing students. No district gave priority to students due to race, income, or other nonachievement characteristics. But because applicants would be randomly selected either to participate or to serve in a nonparticipating control group, districts were asked not to recruit those students required to attend a summer program due to poor grades or the threat of grade retention. Students for whom the district required attendance at a summer program due to poor grades or as a condition of rising into fourth grade could attend the summer programs we studied (or other programs offered in the districts), but were not eligible to participate in our study because they could not be randomly placed into the control group.

Districts and district partners recruited eligible students in multiple ways during spring of 2013: flyers sent home in backpacks, mailers sent to homes, phone calls to parents or guardians, conversations with the students themselves, and events at schools. A marketing firm that The Wallace Foundation hired conducted focus groups with parents in a few cities in the study to determine which messages about summer programs would resonate with them and helped create language for recruiting materials. Flyers and other materials advertised the benefits of receiving academic instruction over the summer while having fun in a camp-like atmosphere with activities like swimming, rock climbing, and the arts. Interested parents filled out an application and signed a consent form to participate in the lottery, the program over two summers (if selected), and the study. Demand for the program was strong across the five districts—5,639 eligible third-grade students applied[1]—and all districts exceeded recruitment goals.

In April and May 2013, RAND randomized students in each district. Across the districts, 3,194 students were assigned to the treatment group (57 percent), and 2,445 (43 percent) were assigned to the control group.[2] The number of students in the study varied by district. In each district, families with students assigned to the control group were given a list of other low-cost or free summer recreation programs in the community. In one district, control group families were also offered a $500 voucher to cover the cost of participation in at least two weeks of a recreational program offered by certain community-based organizations.

As Table 3.1 demonstrates, the students who participated in the study are largely nonwhite and low-income. Across the districts, 47 percent of students in the study were African American and 40 percent Hispanic, and a large majority (89 percent) were FRPL-eligible, an indicator of low family income (see Table 3.1). Overall, 31 percent were English language learners, but Dallas had a much higher proportion, at 59 percent. Across the districts, 10 percent of students had special education needs, as indicated by having an individualized education plan (IEP). The proportion of students with an IEP ranged from 5 percent in Dallas to 17 percent in Pittsburgh. As expected from a random selection process, characteristics are very similar between the treatment and control groups.[3]

In addition, approximately 42 percent of students in the study had scored at the lowest level in either language arts or mathematics or both on the relevant 2013 spring state test—but there were wide variations across districts, with Rochester at 81 percent and Duval at 12 percent. This may be partly due to the varying difficulty of tests from state to state or to the different cut points states use to assign students to levels, but it is also due to choices the districts made about who was eligible to apply. In Duval, students scoring at the lowest level on the state reading assessment were mandated to attend a separate summer program and were thus not eligible to participate in the study.

---

[1]   Subsequent to randomization, two parents withdrew consent for their children's data to be included in our analyses.

[2]   Please see online Appendix A for an explanation of how we selected proportions of students to assign to treatment and control groups.

[3]   Tables in the online appendix show the comparability between the treatment and control groups with respect to background characteristics.

Table 3.1
Demographic Profile of All Study Students, by District

District	Number of Students in the Study	African American (%)	Hispanic (%)	Asian (%)	White (%)	FRPL (%)	English Language Learner (%)	Lowest-Achieving* (%)	IEP (%)
Boston	957	42	41	6	8	NA	30	24	15
Dallas	2,056	19	77	1	1	95	59	43	5
Duval	888	79	5	1	12	87	3	12	8
Pittsburgh	656	70	3	3	17	83	7	39	17
Rochester	1080	65	22	4	8	82	16	81	15
Total	**5,637****	**47**	**40**	**3**	**7**	**89**	**31**	**42**	**10**

SOURCE: District student-level data from school year 2012–2013.

NOTES: Racial and ethnic categories may not add to 100 percent since "other" is not shown.

* Lowest-achieving is defined as students scoring at the lowest level on either the spring 2013 mathematics or reading state tests.

** Two students initially randomized are not represented in this table due to withdrawal of parental consent to use the students' data for this study.

Study Student Attendance in Summer Programs

Summer attendance data and student survey data regarding their activities during the summer provide insights into the activities of control students over the summer, which is important to consider when examining the effects of these programs. The student survey also sheds light on the control group students' summer experiences, which helps to make meaning of the difference in near-term outcomes between the treatment and control groups.

Attendance in the District Summer Programs

Among the 3,194 students in the treatment group, 2,515 attended one or more days of the district 2013 summer programs (79 percent of the treatment group) and 679 students (21 percent of the treatment group) never attended. Table 3.2 displays attendance patterns by district. This overall no-show rate is lower than we observed in these programs for summers 2011 and 2012. No-show rates in summer 2013 ranged from a

Table 3.2
Attendance Rates Across Districts

District	Number of Students in Treatment Group	No-Shows* (Percentage of Students)	Average Attendance Among All Treatment Group Students (Percentage of Days Attended)	Average Attendance** for Students Attending at Least One Day	Attendance Range by Site (Percentage of Days Attended for Students Who Attended at Least One Day)
Boston	574	17	67	80	70–92
Dallas	1,029	27	51	70	61–80
Duval	534	32	56	83	71–88
Pittsburgh	410	19	56	69	65–71
Rochester	647	8	64	69	68–72
Total	3,194	21	58	74	

SOURCE: District summer 2013 attendance data.

* No-shows are the percentage of students who did not attend a single day of the program.

** Average attendance is the percentage of days attended by students who attended one or more days.

low of 8 percent in Rochester to a high of 32 percent in Duval. When we include these no-show students, attendance of treatment students ranged from attending, on average, 51 percent of the days of the summer program in Dallas to 67 percent in Boston. When we look only at students who attended at least one day, students attended most regularly in Duval, with students on average attending 83 percent of the time. In Pittsburgh and Rochester, students attended, on average, 69 percent of the time. We also observed variance in attendance within districts across sites. For instance, in Boston, district average daily attendance was 80 percent, but attendance rates by site ranged from 70 to 92 percent. Across the districts, among the 2,445 students in the control group, 114 (5 percent of the control group) were accidentally allowed to attend one or more days of the summer program.

Attendance in Other Summer Programs

It appears that for many students, the district summer programs provided a structured learning experience they otherwise would not have experienced. Table 3.3 shows that a far larger percentage of treatment students reported attending a camp or summer program (81 percent)[4] compared with the control group (42 percent). Treatment students were far more likely to report reading and writing at camp or summer school compared to control group students. However, 30 percent of control students reported going to a camp where there was reading or writing and 25 percent reported attending a camp that incorporated mathematics.

Treatment status does not appear to have influenced students' reading-at-home habits over the summer. Approximately 85 percent of students in the study reported reading at home at least a few times over the summer, and there were no substantial differences between treatment and control group students.

---

[4]   When we checked treatment group responses against attendance records, we found high, though not perfect, consistency between those records and student reports.

Table 3.3
Summer 2013 Student Survey Responses

	Treatment Group Respondents		Control Group Respondents	
	N	Percentage	N	Percentage
This last summer, I went to camp or summer school				
Did not go to camp or summer school	546	18.7	1,270	57.7
Went for a few days	238	8.1	125	5.7
Went for one week	154	5.3	111	5.0
Went for a few weeks	728	24.9	253	11.5
Went for at least a month	1,256	43.0	442	20.1
I did reading and writing at my camp or summer school this last summer				
Did not go to camp or summer school	544	18.8	1,269	58.6
No	168	5.8	230	10.6
Yes	2,179	75.4	665	30.7
I did mathematics at my camp or summer school this last summer				
Did not go to camp or summer school	545	18.8	1,272	58.7
No	185	6.4	363	16.7
Yes	2,169	74.8	533	24.6
At home this last summer, read a book or a magazine				
Never	370	12.7	321	14.7
A few times this summer	1,563	53.6	1,159	52.9
At least once a week	986	33.8	710	32.4
Composite Survey Variables				
Attended camp with mathematics for at least "a few weeks"				
No	1,060	36.0	1,785	81.0
Yes	1,861	64.0	415	19.0
Attended camp with reading for at least "a few weeks"				
No	1,055	36.0	1,682	77.0
Yes	1,863	64.0	511	23.0
Attended camp for at least "a few weeks"				
No	938	32.0	1,506	68.0
Yes	1,984	68.0	695	32.0

NOTE: Not all students answered each of the four survey questions. Thus, the sum of respondents for each item is not always equal.

CHAPTER FOUR

How Did Implementation of the Summer Programs Vary?

In this chapter, we provide a brief overview of each district's program and describe some of the variation in implementation we observed in summer 2013. As described in Chapter One, each of the district's programs had the following features in common: a minimum of three hours of academic instruction from certified teachers per day for at least five weeks in the summer; free programming, including meals and transportation; a combination of academics and enrichment; and small class sizes. Beyond those requirements, each of the districts created a unique summer program. As shown in Table 4.1 and the rest of this chapter, the programs varied in several ways, including by management structure, number of sites serving students within the district, and whether the programs we studied served students in other grades.

The Summer Learning Programs

Boston Summer Learning Project

Boston's Summer Learning Project (SLP) was a partnership between Boston Public Schools (BPS) and an intermediary organization, Boston After School and Beyond. Staff members from both organizations co-managed the program. A distinctive feature of the Boston program was its goal of providing students unique enrichment opportunities alongside its focus on improving students' academic achievement, with the aim of improving students' social-emotional skills. For example, Boston was the only district that provided academic and enrichment teacher training on students' social-emotional competencies.

While the overarching program encompassed multiple grades, the ten sites that participated in the study exclusively served students who were rising from third into fourth grade during summer 2013. These sites were small, ranging from as few as one classroom of students per site to as many as six classrooms. Across the sites, 574 students were admitted to SLP in summer 2013.

Boston's program was unique among the study districts in that the summer sites are operated primarily by community-based organizations (CBOs) rather than the school district. In partnership with the district, CBO leaders hired a district staff

Table 4.1
Summer 2013 Program Characteristics

	Boston	Dallas	Duval	Pittsburgh	Rochester
Name of summer program included in the study	SLP	Thriving Minds Summer Camp	Super Summer Academy	Summer Dreamers Academy	Rochester Summer Scholars
Program leader(s)	Boston After School and Beyond with BPS	Dallas Independent School District with Big Thought	Duval County Public Schools	Pittsburgh Public Schools	Rochester City School District
Number of sites serving study students	10	10	10	4	1, organized into three "houses"
Program served other grades	No	Yes	Yes	Yes	No
Job titles of adults managing the sites	• Site coordinator (BPS employee) • CBO representatives	• Principal • Assistant principal • Big Thought site manager • Counselor • Data clerk • Office manager	• Principal • Assistant principal • Counselor • Data clerk • Coaches	• Director • Behavior coach • Curriculum coaches • Activity director • Operations managers • Special-education teachers	• Principal • Assistant principals • Site coordinators • Behavior specialists • Curriculum coaches • Special-education consultants • Bilingual consultants
Number of days	25–30	23	29	25	25
Hours of program	Varied: typically seven-hour days.	8 a.m.–5 p.m.	8:15–3:45 p.m.	8:30 a.m.–4 p.m.	7:30 a.m.–3:30 p.m.
Program structure	Varied by site. Typically academics in the morning and enrichment in the afternoon.	Students rotated through sections of academics and enrichment throughout the day	Students rotated through sections of academics and enrichment throughout the day.	Academics in the morning, enrichment in the afternoon.	Academics in the morning, enrichment in the afternoons. Writing offered during the afternoons as well.
Language arts curriculum	American Reading Company	National Geographic Reading Expeditions	District-developed	National Geographic Summer Central	National Geographic Habitats and Forces in Motion
Mathematics curriculum	VMath Summer Adventure	VMath Summer Adventure	Summer Success Math	Number Worlds	VMath Summer Adventure

Table 4.1—Cont.

	Boston	Dallas	Duval	Pittsburgh	Rochester
Enrichment	Varied by site: • Tennis • Sailing • Nature walks • Ropes course • Archery • Arts and crafts • Swimming • Boat building	• Dance • Music • Physical education • Theater • Visual Arts	Varied by site: • Dance • Music • Physical education • Theater • Visual arts • Arts and crafts	Varied by site: • Fencing • Music • Science • Visual arts • Water polo	Varied by house: • Cooking • Dance • Rock climbing • Sand sports/Swimming

member (typically a teacher) to serve as site coordinator to oversee the daily operations of the site and to support teachers. The site coordinator was responsible for setting the daily schedule, recruiting and hiring teachers, taking student attendance, and (depending on the site) arranging bus transportation for students with a private bus contractor. CBO directors, meanwhile, hired and managed enrichment staff, developed the enrichment programming, oversaw the facilities (in many cases), and were on site throughout the summer. Seven of the ten study sites hosted at least the academic classes in BPS school buildings. In these sites, academic teachers typically taught students mathematics and language arts in the morning hours and CBO staff led students in enrichment activities (either on or off campus) in the afternoon. These activities varied based on CBO partners—some students were taught tennis (three sites); others took sailing, boat building, and swimming (two sites); others rotated through a series of camp-like activities in the woods, including archery, hiking, ropes courses, and swimming (three sites); and some students engaged in typical afterschool activities, such as arts and crafts and games (two sites).

The ten summer learning sites operated for at least 25 days, though two sites offered 30 days of programming (the sixth week being enrichment only). Each site was expected to offer 120 minutes of reading instruction and 60 minutes of mathematics instruction per day. The district selected the *VMath Summer Adventure* curriculum. Teachers were also provided *Showtime* materials to supplement *VMath*. The district selected the *American Reading Company* (ARC) curriculum for language arts, a project-based learning program in which students research a chosen topic using nonfiction texts tailored for each student's reading level. Each CBO chose its own ARC theme that linked to its enrichment offerings. For instance, students at the tennis sites studied the human body. Students at one of the nature sites studied ecosystems and chose to research woodlands or wetlands. Each student created a self-published nonfiction book on a selected topic within the site theme, such as the life cycle of the frog or the human circulatory system. In addition, the ARC curriculum included a 100-book challenge and teachers were expected to set aside 30 minutes per day for independent reading of student-selected fiction or nonfiction texts.

Dallas Thriving Minds Summer Camp

The Thriving Minds Summer Camp launched in 2010 to support both failing elementary students and students participating in 21st Century after-school programs in the Dallas Independent School District. As such, it has been co-led by the district and Big Thought, a community nonprofit organization that supports student learning through the arts. The goals of the program have been to help students improve academically, to provide arts enrichment to students who would otherwise not have access, and to boost students' self-esteem so they would think of themselves with a "growth mindset."

In 2013, elementary students at 81 schools were eligible to apply for a spot in one of ten Thriving Minds Summer Camps. Each of these sites served three categories of students in grades K–5: (1) students failing their classes, (2) students participating in the 21st Century after-school programs, and (3) rising fourth-grade students in this research study. Across the ten sites, 1,029 rising fourth-grade treatment students were originally admitted to the Thriving Minds Summer Camp as a part of the research study. One student subsequently opted out, leaving 1,028 in the Dallas treatment group.

The school district and Big Thought provided overall program management. For example, the district developed a summer principal handbook listing summer policies and documenting procedures. District leaders coordinated with the transportation and food services department. Together, the district and Big Thought selected the curriculum and distributed curricular materials and other supplies. Both recruited students, and they jointly developed a daily schedule and managed the summer sites. Both organizations also provided professional development to the teachers. Big Thought took the lead on planning the enrichment component and hiring those instructors.

Each of the ten sites was led by a summer principal who served as an assistant principal during the school year. Assistant principals, Big Thought site managers, counselors, data clerks, and office managers supported these summer principals. These building leaders hired teachers, adjusted the schedules to fit the sites, developed procedures for arrival and dismissal, observed instruction, and managed the program each day.

The program spanned 23 school days, ran from 8 a.m. to 5 p.m. each day, and was hosted exclusively on district public school campuses. Academics and enrichment blocks were dispersed throughout the day.

Program leaders selected *VMath Summer Adventure* to build computational fluency with a strong focus on building mathematical vocabulary and communicating both orally and in writing to justify the reasonableness of mathematical answers and processes. They also selected National Geographic's *Reading Expeditions* language arts curriculum to provide literacy instruction through grade-level content in science and social studies, with a strong emphasis on development of nonfiction reading skills and strategies. The goal of the program was to boost literacy skills through the use of engaging, grade-level, informational text.

Both district-certified teachers and community artists taught enrichment blocks in Dallas. Students participated in physical education, visual arts, music, dance, and theater. They cycled through traditional blocks of instruction in these subjects and experienced "studio time" at the end of the day in which they could work independently and in groups to create art.

Duval Super Summer Academy

Duval's program was centrally managed by the district, Duval County Public Schools, in coordination with the school-year principals of the host sites. Duval's program originated in the district's elementary schools that were in "Turnaround" status per federal No Child Left Behind Act designation due to persistently low student performance on state assessments. With Wallace funding, the program expanded to serve all 50

Title I elementary schools in the district that sent students to ten Super Summer Academy sites. While the study only included students rising from third into fourth grade during summer 2013, the sites also served students moving into grades kindergarten through fifth grade and hosted between 19 and 32 classrooms of students in these grades. Across the ten sites, 535 rising fourth-grade students were originally admitted by lottery to the Super Summer Academy treatment group. One student subsequently opted out, leaving 534 in the Duval treatment group.

District central office staff selected the curriculum and materials, organized transportation and meals, selected students, and recruited teachers. Principals of host schools developed their own summer theme, created a daily schedule, and helped select teachers for the site. Principals, with the help of assistant principals in most sites, were responsible for the daily operation of the program. Sites had additional staff to support teachers, students, and parents—including curriculum coaches, a part-time counselor, and office staff.

In summer 2013, sites operated for 29 days, from 8:15 a.m. to 3:45 p.m., and were required to offer at least 90 minutes of language arts, 60 minutes of mathematics, 45 minutes of science, and 45 minutes of a computer-based learning class per day. In 2013, most sites exceeded the required amount of instructional time for reading and mathematics.

The district used *Summer Success Math*, which provides daily practice in operations, patterns and algebra, vocabulary, geometry, and measurement, a daily independent practice activity (which includes a word problem) and games. For reading, the school district adapted its own curricular content based on Florida history—the topical focus of the upcoming fourth-grade social science curriculum. Students were to practice reading comprehension strategies such as compare and contrast, using text features, and creating timelines for nonfiction texts about Florida history, including student newspapers produced by the state of Florida, one National Geographic book, and a set of online articles selected by district curriculum developers.

Sites selected their own enrichment classes, typically art, music, dance, and physical education. Enrichment was offered by district teachers (all sites), CBO after-school partner staff (two sites), and professional teaching artists (two sites). Students also participated in an end-of-program field trip to DisneyQuest and a culminating production such as a performance or a play to which families were invited.

Pittsburgh Summer Dreamers Academy

Summer Dreamers Academy (SDA) was a summer learning camp managed by the Pittsburgh Public Schools central office staff. Its goals were to encourage a passion for learning and exploration and to improve students' academic achievement. The program, which began in 2010 as a camp for students entering sixth to eighth grade, expanded its eligibility criteria in 2011 to include all K–8 students in the district. The program continued through summer 2013 with a small amount of funding from the district's Title I allocation, along with grant support from local and national foundations (The Fund for Excellence in Pittsburgh Public Schools, Walmart Foundation, and The Wallace Foundation).

The 2013 program served more than 2,000 students in grades K–8. Students in K–5 attended the program in four school district buildings. All students entering sixth, seventh, and eighth grades attended camp at a fifth location. Across the four SDA sites, 410 rising fourth-grade students were originally admitted to the treatment group via lottery.

Each winter the district central office team hired staff who planned for and managed the camps. This included contracting with 21 community-based organizations to provide enrichment programming and hiring camp counselors who would assist teachers and students during academic class sessions in the summer.

A seven-member Camp Leadership Team was responsible for daily operations at each site. These teams consisted of a camp director, two camp operations managers, two curriculum coaches, a behavior management coach, and an activity specialist. In 2013, the program operated Monday through Friday, 8:30 a.m. to 4 p.m., for five weeks.

Sites were to provide students 90-minute blocks of mathematics and language arts. The literacy block consisted of the reading curriculum based on the National Geographic *Summer Central* content and additional reading interventions used by the district during the school year. Students focused on phonics, fluency, vocabulary, and comprehension. The mathematics block was based on the McGraw-Hill *Number Worlds* curriculum, along with problem-solving activities and mathematics-related board games, with the goal that students improve number sense, basic mathematics facts, and computation.

Twenty-one CBOs provided 26 different enrichment opportunities for various groups of students scheduled throughout the day. After lunch and recess, students participated in two blocks of enrichment activities with options such as judo, fencing, science, and visual and performance art. Additional activities occurred once a week, such as visits from the Carnegie Public Library and trips to the Promise Store (an incentive strategy in which students earned play money during the week and could buy prizes at the end of the week). There were also special events, such as a Scholastic Book Fair in Week Two, and culminating camp events in Week Five, such as a music performance or an art showcase.

Rochester Summer Scholars

The Rochester summer learning program was managed by the Rochester City School District. First known as Rochester's Summer Enrichment Program, it originated as an academic half-day summer-school program for the lowest-performing students at each grade level who might have had to repeat the school year. With Wallace funding, the district augmented the program by offering afternoon enrichment activities to students entering fourth grade.

In the second year of the study, which was still prior to the launch of the randomized controlled trial, the district branded the summer program as the Rochester

Summer Scholars program to differentiate it from the traditional summer school program offered to all students in the district. The district hired a new person to oversee this program, moved it to a separate large school building, expanded the number of seats offered to rising fourth-grade students, expanded the hours of the summer school day, added enrichment activities, and increased the number of staff. The district hired one principal to run the program and three assistant principals, each of whom helped manage one of the three "houses" within the building where Rochester Summer Scholars was hosted. Staff included positive behavior support consultants, instructional coaches, academic teachers, enrichment teachers (from district and community-based organizations), enrichment assistant principals, and paraprofessionals.

In 2013, the program operated for 25 days, with 24 days of instruction. The program was split into three "houses" and the district intended for each house to offer 80 minutes of language arts, 80 minutes of mathematics, and 40 minutes of targeted reading instruction. Students participated in two enrichment blocks each day; the district aimed for each of these to be 80 minutes, for 160 minutes of enrichment activities per day.

Program leaders used a combination of purchased and locally developed curriculum. They designed a mathematics curriculum based on *VMath Summer Adventure*. The curriculum aimed to provide students practice in basic skills, preview instruction for the fourth-grade mathematics curriculum (particularly fractions), and provide varied opportunities to practice skills by playing a math game each day. District curriculum writers also designed a reading curriculum based on two kits released by National Geographic, *Habitats* and *Forces in Motion*. The aim of the curriculum was to provide students with instruction in reading strategies for nonfiction text and to expose students to fourth-grade science content. Each day, students also rotated into small-group targeted instruction for reading using either *Phonics Boost* or *Phonics Blitz* to develop reading skills. During this block, students who were more advanced readers participated in groups aimed at sustaining or improving fluency and comprehension. Afternoon writing teachers designed and implemented a nonfiction writing class that students attended every three to four days, depending on their afternoon enrichment schedule.

The central office staff member coordinated enrichment activities offered by CBOs as well as district staff. Enrichment activities, which varied by house and occurred on a rotating schedule, included rock climbing, culinary arts, swimming, physical education, art, music, African dance and drumming, theater, dance, and yoga.

Cross-District Program Implementation

We observed variation in program enactment as well as design, across districts and within districts. Because some of this variation—such as differences in student attendance and time spent on academic instruction—could have affected student outcomes, we highlight these factors here.

Amount of Instruction Received

Each district was asked to run its program for five weeks. All did, but days of the program ranged from 23 in Dallas to 30 in Duval and in some of the Boston sites. Hours of the program day varied less, ranging from 7 to 8 hours each day.

In almost all the districts, teachers spent less time on instruction than the district had intended. For example, one district expected students to receive 38 hours each of language arts and mathematics during the program. Our observations indicated that just 30 hours of reading and 34 hours of mathematics were actually offered. One common factor that contributed to this discrepancy was teachers' tendency to start classes late and end them early. Some site-specific decisions also affected instructional hours: One site instituted a recess in the second week; another decided to start the first class at 9:30 a.m. instead of 9:15 a.m.

In addition to classes starting late or ending early, the gap between intended and actual instructional time further widened due to noninstructional minutes *during* class time. When we recorded (via classroom observation time logs) instructional and noninstructional minutes (e.g., off-topic conversations, bathroom breaks, snacks, long interludes for disciplinary actions) we found that students would receive an average of 25 hours of reading and 28 hours of mathematics over the course of the summer (assuming these students had perfect attendance).

Student absences further reduced the hours of instruction they received. As described in the prior section, average daily attendance across all the districts for students who attended at least one day was 74 percent (ranging from 69 to 83 percent). In three districts, 13 to 19 percent of these students attended only five or fewer days. Average daily attendance declined over the course of the five- or six-week summer program in every district. In addition, 21 percent of students in the treatment group were no-shows and never attended a day of the program.

After combining shortened class hours, noninstructional class time, student absences, and no-show rates, the average instructional time for a typical student was 23 hours in language arts and 17 hours in mathematics. However, there was variation across districts. The typical student in the treatment group received as few as 13 hours of language arts instruction to as many as 30 hours. In mathematics, the typical student in the treatment group received as few as 15 hours to as many as 21 hours. Of course, students who actually attended for at least one day had higher average instructional hours. Across the districts, students who attended at least one day received an average of 29 hours of language arts instruction and 21 hours of mathematics instruction.

Instructional Quality

Processes for recruiting and hiring teachers varied, but none of the districts conducted interviews or observed teachers before hiring them. According to site leaders and coaches whom RAND interviewed, the quality of teachers and instruction in summer 2013 was mixed. Some site leaders reported that their group of academic teachers was "phenomenal" while others noted some teacher weaknesses. In our classroom observations, we detected a range of instructional quality. On our 10-point index, the typical observation rated around 5 in reading and mathematics, with a range from 2.6 to 7.1.

Some teachers had not recently taught either third or fourth grade. In one district, only 42 percent of the academic teachers had taught either the third or fourth grade in the previous year. Coaches noted in interviews with us that these teachers sometimes struggled with the curriculum, communicating at the appropriate level, and managing behavior appropriately. In most districts and sites, teachers were departmentalized, which enabled them to focus on one subject and curriculum. Over the course of the program, most teachers used the reading and mathematics curricular materials as intended and most attended professional development sessions that explained the curricular materials.

Summer class sizes were small across the districts, ranging from eight to 14 students on average. Despite the small class sizes, however, academic teachers reported that it was challenging to teach students with such a range of skill levels. In most of the districts, students varied in their knowledge and skill levels and teachers were asked to differentiate their instruction accordingly. Teachers we interviewed reported that there was insufficient guidance in the lesson plans on how to target instruction to student needs and insufficient materials to support modifications to the curriculum, either for remediation or acceleration. A majority of teachers did not have prior school-year data about their students' skill levels on district or state tests or their IEP plans.

Site Discipline and Order

Finally, maintaining order and discipline in the classroom proved difficult in two of the districts. In these districts, half of the surveyed teachers agreed that a great deal of learning time was wasted because of time spent disciplining students. Half also reported that students were bullied or harassed by other students at least once a week. Many disruptive incidents occurred during transitions, such as bathroom breaks and snack times. According to teacher surveys, some summer sites had not established a clear and effective method for handling student discipline. By contrast, few teachers in the other three districts reported problems with student behavior.

In the following chapters, we estimate the short-term effect of being admitted to a summer program. Then, given the substantial variation in the implementation of the summer programs, we also examine whether implementation factors were related to student outcomes.

CHAPTER FIVE

What Were the Near-Term Effects of the Summer Programs?

The goal of this study is to identify program effects on student learning in math and reading and explore whether the program contributed to students' social-emotional outcomes. With the first results from fall 2013 assessments now analyzed, we can demonstrate that the summer learning programs made a significant difference in students' performance in mathematics. We report on those findings here. Later reports will examine whether the single summer program continues to influence student achievement at the end of the school year and whether offering a second consecutive summer of programming improves these outcomes.

The Programs Had a Positive Effect on Fall 2013 Mathematics Achievement

The summer programs had a significant positive effect on students' mathematics achievement when compared to students in the control group. This held true when we analyzed results for different sets of mathematics skills: concepts and communication, operations and computation, and process and application. The treatment students outperformed the control students on all three of these assessment subscales.

The tables in this section present effect sizes using two analytic approaches described above: the effect on students who actually attended the program (TOT analysis) and the effect on all students who enrolled in the program, whether they attended or not (ITT analysis).

As shown in Table 5.1, the average effect of attending the summer programs across the five school districts was 0.11 in mathematics, which is statistically significant.[1] The ITT estimate is 0.09 and also is statistically significant. When we look at each district individually (not shown in table), each district treatment effect is positive

---

[1] An effect size quantifies the difference between two groups. We report effect sizes in standardized units, which are expressed as a fraction of the standard deviation (or spread) of the post-test scores. Using standardized effect sizes enables comparisons of the estimated effects of the summer programs to effects measured in other research studies.

Table 5.1
Effects of Summer Learning Programs on Near-Term Student Outcomes

Average Effect	Mathematics	Reading	Socio-emotional
Attending at least one day (TOT)	0.11*	0.02	0.01
	(0.03)	(0.02)	(0.02)
Being offered a slot in the summer program (ITT)	0.09*	0.01	0.01
	(0.02)	(0.02)	(0.03)

NOTE: Treatment effect estimates are reported in standardized effect sizes; numbers in parentheses are standard errors; * indicates significance at the $p<.05$ level after adjustment for multiple hypothesis tests.

but none of the TOT estimates are statistically significant. In two out of five districts, the ITT estimates (0.08 and 0.13) are statistically significant. Although the other districts' ITT estimates are not significant, it is important to remember that this study was not designed to detect district-specific effects with accuracy. Because the district estimates do not significantly differ from one another, it is reasonable to conclude that all districts contributed to the overall positive finding in mathematics.

The overall mathematics effect size of 0.11 is reasonably large for a five- to six-week intervention. This effect size is slightly larger than average effect sizes measured for other education intervention evaluations. Lipsey et al. (2012) report that across 89 published and unpublished randomized controlled trials examining elementary interventions using a broad-scope standardized test like GMADE, the mean effect size was 0.08 and the median was 0.07.

To help interpret how large an effect of 0.11 is, we can compare it to empirical data on typical mathematics achievement growth during a school year for students this age. Lipsey et al. report that average student growth in mathematics for the full calendar year between the spring of third and fourth grades is 0.52. It is important to remember that our effect represents an advantage of program attendees in mathematics achievement but does not tell us whether these students experienced growth over the summer, the control group experienced loss, or some combination of the two. However, treatment students in our study began the fall 2013 academic year with an advantage over their control group counterparts that appears meaningful relative to typical annual growth. A later phase of this study will investigate whether teachers and students were able to capitalize on this advantage over the course of the school year.

Prior literature on summer learning provides another way to contextualize our findings in mathematics. Two studies of mandatory summer learning programs that included fourth-graders found effect sizes of 0.12 and 0.14 on state standardized tests of mathematics in the following spring (Jacob and Lefgren, 2004; Matsudaira, 2008). Although those estimates are slightly larger than our results, it is not uncommon for nonexperimental studies to estimate larger effect sizes than experiments.

The Programs Had No Discernable Effect on Fall 2013 Reading Achievement

We found no difference between the treatment and the control group students on the fall 2013 reading assessment. As Table 5.1 shows, the overall effect for program attendees on the reading score was 0.02 and was not statistically significant. Additional analyses (not shown in the table) found that treatment students did not demonstrate statistically significant differences in outcomes compared to the control students in any of the districts. Some other evaluations of summer programs have found impacts on reading outcomes; others have not. Three recent randomized controlled trials have found significant effects of reading summer programs (Chaplin and Capizzano, 2006) and reading-at-home programs (James Kim, 2006; Kim and White, 2008) that included students in the same age range as our study.[2] However, other evaluations of read-at-home programs have not found statistically significant effects in reading (Jimmy Kim, 2004; Kim and Guryan, 2010; Wilkins et al., 2012; White et al., 2013).

The Programs Had No Discernable Effect on Fall 2013 Social-Emotional Outcomes

Finally, as Table 5.1 also shows, students who attended the summer program for at least one day or who were admitted to the summer programs did no better on measures of social and emotional competencies than students in the control group. Although some district leaders in the summer learning study anticipated that their programs would have a positive effect of this kind, most did not provide explicit instruction or programming designed to improve students' social and emotional competencies. Only one district provided teacher training in this area. The effect estimate in this district (0.10, not shown in table) was positive and larger than in the other districts, but not statistically significant. Only one other study of summer learning has tracked nonacademic outcomes (Chapin and Capizzano, 2006), and its authors did not find effects of the program on academic self-perception or social behaviors.

Student Demographics and Characteristics Were Not Related to Near-Term Outcomes

We ran additional analyses to examine whether three specific groups of participants experienced larger or smaller treatment effects than students not in those groups. The groups were English language learners, students eligible for free or reduced-price lunch, and students who scored below the median of our sample on prior achievement tests.

---

[2] Unlike our methods, these studies did not apply corrections for multiple hypothesis tests.

The findings were that, relative to the control group, treatment effects for these students were approximately the same as those for other students in the treatment group.

Lack of Service Contrast Is Unlikely to Have Caused the Study to Underestimate Program Effects

As discussed earlier, the experiment compares the performance of students in the district programs to a control group that was denied admission to those programs. If a large number of control group students attended alternative summer programs that included effective academic instruction, both groups might perform similarly in the fall even if the district programs were effective. In other words, if the control group received effective instruction over the summer, it could cause us to underestimate the effects of summer programs. However, analysis of student survey data suggested this was not the case. The student survey asked all students in the study about their activities over the summer. We grouped students into categories based on whether they reported attending a summer program or camp with academic instruction for at least a few weeks. In this analysis, we estimated treatment effects for treatment group students who reported attending a program with an academic focus and control group students who reported attending a program with an academic focus relative to a comparison group of control group students who reported they did not attend a program with an academic focus. For both mathematics and reading, models estimated a positive effect for treatment group students who reported attending a program or camp with academics, but not for control group students who reported attending such a program or camp. Although this analysis did not produce causal estimates of the effects of the district programs or other programs, it did help to alleviate the concern that control group students attended academic programs that would result in this study underestimating the effects of the district summer programs.

In the next chapter, we turn to exploratory analyses that examine how features of the programs, as well as attendance and dosage, relate to the near-term outcomes experienced by participants.

CHAPTER SIX

What Aspects of Summer Programs Are Related to Positive Outcomes?

Summer program leaders want to know what aspects of programming influence student outcomes. Because this study gathered program implementation data, we are able to conduct analyses to examine how programmatic features are related to the programs' effects on student outcomes. We examined seven characteristics of summer programs that we expected might increase the summer programs' effects on admitted students:

- attendance, or the number of days a student attended the program
- dosage, or the amount of instructional hours a student received
- relative opportunity for individual attention, which combines dosage and class size
- quality of instruction in students' mathematics and language arts classrooms
- appropriateness of the curriculum
- teacher's prior teaching experiences with the sending or receiving grade level
- site discipline and order.

The goal of these analyses was to determine what aspects of a summer learning program led to improved student outcomes. However, these analyses were challenging because students were not randomly assigned to experience different features of the programs. For any program feature, it is possible that students experiencing the feature (say, high attendance or high-quality instruction) have different backgrounds or abilities than those who do not, and these differences could bias estimates of the feature's effects. However, we did not find evidence that students with different prior achievement levels were unevenly distributed across implementation features. For example, we did not find that students who attended more regularly were higher performing on pretreatment achievement measures. Nonetheless, student differences may still exist. Thus, we cannot say with certainty that results from these analyses are caused by the programmatic features themselves rather than other factors.

With those caveats in mind, these results provide the best available evidence regarding the relationship between programmatic features and student outcomes. We found five instances where these factors had a statistically significant association with mathematics or reading outcomes: attendance, dosage, quality of instruction, teacher qualifications, and student discipline and order (Table 6.1).[1] Taken together, the findings suggest that instructional time matters for mathematics outcomes and that instructional quality and orderliness of the environment matter for reading outcomes.

Strong Attendance and More Instructional Time Were Associated with Better Mathematics Outcomes

We expected that attendance would affect student outcomes. To test this assumption, we collected daily attendance data and found that student attendance varied by district and even within districts by program site, as reported in Chapter Three. When we analyzed the relationship between student attendance and program effects, we found that increased attendance was associated with higher mathematics scores. In addition to examining the linear relationship between attendance and achievement, we examined categories of attendance in order to provide practical guidance to program operators. We split students into three categories of attendance—no-shows (0 days attended), low (1 to 21 days attended), and high (22 or more days attended)—and ran statistical models to compare the outcomes of each of these groups to the control group. (Online Appendix C explains the method by which we determined the appropriate cut points for these categories.) We found that the stronger the attendance, the better students performed on the fall 2013 mathematics test (Table 6.2). While the estimates in reading trend upward with increased attendance, we did not find statistically significant relationships between attendance and reading achievement across the districts.

We also examined the actual hours of instruction a student received in mathematics and in language arts. This measure took into account students' daily attendance and the estimated number of hours of language arts and mathematics instruction each student's class received on a daily basis. (See online Appendix C for how we constructed this dosage measure.)

Table 6.1
Implementation Factors Significantly and Positively Correlated with Student Achievement

Implementation Factor	Mathematics Achievement	Reading Achievement
Attendance	Positive association	No association
Dosage	Positive association	No association
Instructional quality	No association	Positive association
Grade level experience of teacher	No association	Positive association
Site orderliness	No association	Positive association

---

[1]   In these exploratory analyses, we do not apply corrections for multiple hypothesis tests.

Table 6.2
Relationships Between Student Attendance and Near-Term Student Outcomes in Mathematics and Reading

Attendance	Mathematics		Reading	
	N	Estimate (std. error)	N	Estimate (std. error)
No-show	588	−0.01 (0.03)	584	−0.03 (0.03)
Low	1,054	0.07** (0.02)	1,057	−0.01 (0.02)
High	1,279	0.14*** (0.02)	1,261	0.04 (0.02)

NOTES: Treatment effect estimates are reported in standardized effect sizes; numbers in parenthesis are standard errors; * indicates significance at the $p<.05$ level; ** indicates significance at the $p<.01$ level; ***indicates significance at the $<.001$ level. N values sum to the number of treatment group students with post-test scores in the respective subject.

We found that increased hours of instruction were also associated with higher mathematics scores. We also examined categories of instructional hour dosage by classifying treatment students into groups who never attended (no-shows) and who received low (more than 0 to less than 13 hours), medium (13 to less than 26 hours), and high (26 hours or more) dosage.[2] Statistical models compared the outcomes of these subgroups to control students. We found that, in mathematics, higher dosages of instruction were associated with higher performance on the fall 2013 standardized assessments (Table 6.3). Students who received the medium dosage and those who received a high dosage of mathematics instruction scored statistically significantly higher than control students, with the higher dosage students obtaining the larger advantage over control students. Similar to our attendance analysis, we did not find a consistent, significant relationship between higher dosages of instruction and reading outcomes, though estimates in reading trend upward with increased dosage.

In summary, as reported in Chapter Five, the experimental analysis found that the programs were effective in mathematics. In our implementation analyses discussed here, attendance and instructional hours seem to provide students an even greater achievement boost in mathematics but not in near-term reading or in social-emotional skills. The categorical analysis suggests that program operators may want to aim to develop programs that last at least five weeks and spend 60–90 minutes per day on mathematics.

---

[2] As described in Chapter Four, sites scheduled more time for reading than mathematics. The categories we tested were different in reading than mathematics: low dosage (more than 0 to less than 31 hours); medium dosage (31 to less than 39 hours); and high dosage (39 hours or more).

Table 6.3
Relationships Between Instructional Time and Near-Term Student Outcomes in Mathematics and Reading

	Mathematics		Reading	
Dosage	N	Estimate (std. error)	N	Estimate (std. error)
No-show	588	−0.01 (0.03)	584	−0.03 (0.03)
Low	493	0.05 (0.03)	1,152	−0.01 (0.02)
Medium	1,011	0.10*** (0.02)	493	0.03 (0.03)
High	829	0.16*** (0.03)	673	0.04 (0.03)

NOTES: Treatment effect estimates are reported in standardized effect sizes; numbers in parenthesis are standard errors; * indicates significance at the p<.05 level; ** indicates significance at the p<.01 level; ***indicates significance at the <.001 level. N's sum to the number of treatment group students with posttest scores in the respective subject.

Instructional Quality Was Associated with Positive Reading Outcomes

Because we expected that quality of instruction would be associated with student outcomes, we observed and evaluated instructional quality for each classroom. (See Table 2.2 for our definition of instructional quality.)[3] Our analysis found a positive association between quality of instruction and better student performance in reading. We did not find a relationship between quality of instruction and student performance in mathematics. This finding implies that, while we found positive results for mathematics regardless of our measure of instructional quality, reading outcomes may have been more sensitive to instructional quality.

Having a Teacher with Relevant Grade-Level Experience Was Associated with Positive Reading Outcomes

We expected that summer program teachers who had just taught third- or fourth-graders during the prior school year would be more effective because they would be knowledgeable about both the academic standards for fourth grade and the appropriate pedagogy for this age group. Across the school districts, 56 percent of the language arts teachers and 66 percent of mathematics teachers had taught either third or fourth grade in the previous school year. Our analysis found a positive, statistically significant

---

[3] For mathematics and language arts instructional quality measures, we assigned a rating to classrooms even though such ratings are prone to large error because of the small number of observations. Online Appendix B describes how we attempted to make these measures as accurate as possible, given available resources. A classroom score was attributed to each student who attended that class.

association between prior teaching experience and reading outcomes. The mathematics treatment effects were insensitive to teachers' grade-level experience.

Orderly Sites Were Associated with Better Reading Outcomes

We also expected that students in more orderly sites would have better outcomes because they and their teachers would be less likely to be distracted by misbehavior. To evaluate student discipline and order in the programs, we created a scale for each site within each district based on teacher survey data. (See Table 2.6 for the items in this scale.) We found that students who attended more orderly sites outperformed control group students in reading. Again, mathematics treatment effects were insensitive to site orderliness.

Other Factors Were Not Associated with Program Effects

Two other factors we tested were not associated with near-term student outcomes:

1. *Opportunity for individual attention* combined dosage (or instructional hours) with class size to test whether more individual attention offered due to smaller classes might improve results. Although we found that the number of hours of instructional time was related to mathematics treatment effects, we did not find a relationship when further combined with class size. This may be because prevailing class sizes across the districts were all fairly small—from an average of eight in Duval to 14 in Pittsburgh.[4]
2. *Teachers' perceptions of the appropriateness of the curriculum*—which teachers rated in terms of reasonable pacing, clarity of curriculum, whether the curriculum addressed the right gaps in student knowledge and skills, and whether it was fun for students—was not related to treatment effects.

The next chapter summarizes our key findings and their implications, along with next steps for the study.

---

[4] To calculate average class size, we applied districts' student-level attendance data to classroom rosters to calculate the average number of students present in each class. Each student in the treatment group who attended one or more days of the summer program was associated with an assigned language arts and mathematics classroom size.

CHAPTER SEVEN

Key Findings and Implications

This study tests whether free, voluntary, district-run summer programs that include academics and enrichment activities benefit low-income elementary students. Because we evaluate five different programs in five different states, we are examining a "proof of concept" rather than the effectiveness of a particular program in a specific locale. We summarize here the key findings of our analysis to date, their implications for school districts considering such programs, some possible explanations for the absence of program impact on reading and social/emotional development, and next steps for the study.

Summer Learning Programs Appear to Serve Community Needs

We found there was strong demand among low-income students and their families for free, voluntary programs that combine academics and enrichment. Each district exceeded its expectations for applications, and the majority of accepted students attended the programs. In addition, these district-run programs provided many students with opportunities for instruction and enrichment that they would not otherwise have had during the summer. Almost 60 percent of the control group, all of whom had applied to the districts' voluntary summer program but were denied admission, reported not attending any kind of summer program or camp over the summer. These families had all received targeted information on other summer learning programs available in their communities.

These findings suggest that urban districts around the country are likely to find strong community interest in full-day, voluntary, district-provided summer learning programs that provide both academic and enrichment experiences for elementary school students at no cost to families.

Students Who Attended the Programs Entered School in the Fall with Stronger Mathematics Skills Than Those Who Did Not

The students in our study who attended the summer programs entered the fall semester with a meaningful advantage in mathematics achievement. Because the vast majority of our study students were low-income, it is likely that this finding would generalize to other low-income, middle elementary–grade students in urban settings.

Our implementation analyses suggest that students who attended more often and who received more instructional hours received the greatest benefit. These results are consistent with theory. Because math is generally thought to be more sensitive to school instruction than reading, increasing the amount of math instruction time and learning should improve student outcomes. Our analyses imply that to maximize benefits for students, districts may want to plan for programs that run five to six weeks and schedule 60–90 minutes of mathematics per day. Because instructional time on task is reduced due to student absences and inefficient use of time inside the day, districts should make special efforts to promote consistent attendance, maintain daily schedules, and ensure teachers maximize instructional time inside the classroom. A later phase of the study will investigate whether these benefits persist throughout the school year.

The Programs Did Not Produce Near-Term Effects in Reading

We did not find differences between the treatment and control groups in reading. The absence of an effect in reading was somewhat surprising because our sample consists primarily of low-income students who, according to the research, lose more ground than their higher-income peers in their reading skills over the summer.

There are several plausible explanations for this result. It could be that control group students did not lose ground, or even improved their reading skills over the summer. We did not use an assessment before the summer that would enable us to examine whether treatment and control groups experienced growth or decline over the summer. It could also be that a five-week summer program did not provide enough dosage to create measurable improvement in reading skills. In our implementation analyses, we do not find that reading outcomes are significantly affected even for students who attended at the highest rates (22 or more days) or received the highest dosage (39 or more hours). Some research has concluded that reading comprehension scores are harder to shift for students in grades higher than second grade than they are for younger students (Wanzek and Vaughn, 2007; Wanzek et al., 2013). These authors speculate that this may be the case because reading expectations for students in the upper-elementary grades often require more cognitively demanding tasks (which are related to word meanings, background knowledge, and understanding of complex text) than expectations for readers in kindergarten through second grade, where goals tend to focus on basic word recognition and lower-level reading comprehension skills. Researchers also conclude that reading scores, particularly reading comprehension, are more susceptible to measurement error than math scores (Cain and Oakhil, 2006; Betjemann et al., 2012; Cutting and Scarborough 2006; Keenan, Betjemann, and Olson, 2008; Morsy, Kieffer, and Snow, 2010; Wanzek and Vaughn, 2007; Wanzek et al., 2013). It could also be that overall instructional quality was simply not high enough to boost reading skills for students who attended the summer program one or more days.

Our implementation analyses suggest that reading outcomes may be sensitive to classroom and site quality. These analyses found that higher-quality instruction, having a teacher with grade-level experience, and attending an orderly site were associated with improved reading outcomes. These findings imply that districts may want to take particular care in selecting reading teachers for summer programming, trying to select the highest-quality reading teachers and those with grade-level experience (in either the sending or receiving grade). Also, methods of establishing an orderly site seem worthy of attention. Establishing clear expectations for student behavior, ensuring consistent application across teachers, and developing methods of maintaining positive student behavior in class may pay off in terms of student achievement in reading.

The Summer Programs Did Not Affect Social-Emotional Outcomes

Treatment students did not receive higher social and emotional competence ratings from their teachers in the fall than control students received. While some district leaders hypothesized that their programs might have a positive effect on social-emotional outcomes, only one district explicitly designed a program with this outcome in mind. As we reported, the effect size estimate in this district was positive and larger than in the other districts, though not statistically significant in the relatively small within-district sample.

These results suggest that districts may need to take specific actions in designing and executing their summer programs if they wish to affect students' social-emotional outcomes in the near term. It may also be that students may need longer exposure to the summer programs to undergo change in their social-emotional development or, as previously mentioned, social and emotional outcomes may result from improved achievement over time. Our analysis after two years of summer participation may shed greater light on these hypotheses.

Next Steps

Our next report, which will be published in summer 2015, will examine the effects of this one summer of programming on students' behavior and achievement throughout the 2013–2014 school year. Subsequent publications will describe the impact of two consecutive years of programming on student outcomes, and examine program costs. Together, these findings will enhance our understanding about how to design and implement summer learning programs, what kind of outcomes to expect from these programs, and whether district investment in these programs is cost effective.

Bibliography

Allington, Richard L., Anne McGill-Franzen, Gregory Camilli, Lunetta Williams, Jennifer Graff, Jacqueline Zeig, Courtney Zmach, and Rhonda Nowak, "Addressing Summer Reading Setback Among Economically Disadvantaged Elementary Students," *Reading Psychology*, Vol. 31, No. 5, October 2010, pp. 411–427.

Augustine, Catherine H., Jennifer Sloan McCombs, Heather L. Schwartz, and Laura Zakaras, *Getting to Work on Summer Learning: Recommended Practices for Success*, Santa Monica, Calif.: RAND Corporation, RR-366-WF, 2013. As of October 31, 2014: http://www.rand.org/pubs/research_reports/RR366.html

Benjamini, Yoav, and Yosef Hochberg, "Controlling the False Discovery Rate: A Practical and Powerful Approach to Multiple Testing," *Journal of the Royal Statistical Society, Series B (Methodological)*, Vol. 57, No. 1, 1995, pp. 289–300.

Betjemann, Rebecca, Janice Keenan, Richard Olson, and John DeFries, "Choice of Reading Comprehension Test Influences the Outcomes of Genetic Analyses," *Scientific Studies of Reading*, Vol. 15, No. 4, 2012, pp. 363–382.

Borman, Geoffrey D., James Benson, and Laura T. Overman, "Families, Schools, and Summer Learning," *Elementary School Journal*, Vol. 106, 2005, pp. 131–150.

Borman, Geoffrey, Michael Goetz, and N. Maritza Dowling, "Halting the Summer Achievement Slide: A Randomized Field Trial of the KindergARTen Summer Camp," *Journal of Education for Students Placed at Risk* (JESPAR), Vol. 14, No. 2, April 2009, pp. 133–147.

Cain, Kate, and Jane Oakhil, "Assessment Matters: Issues in the Measurement of Reading Comprehension," *British Journal of Educational Psychology*, Vol. 76, 2006, pp. 697–708.

Cameron, A. Colin, Jonah B. Gelbach, and Douglas L. Miller, "Bootstrap-Based Improvements for Inference with Clustered Errors," *Review of Economics and Statistics*, Vol. 90, No. 3, 2008, pp. 414–427.

Chaplin, Duncan, and Jeffrey Capizzano, *Impacts of a Summer Learning Program: A Random Assignment Study of Building Educated Leaders for Life* (BELL), Washington, D.C.: Urban Institute, 2006.

Cooper, Harris, Barbara Nye, Kelly Charlton, James Lindsay, and Scott Greathouse, "The Effects of Summer Vacation on Achievement Test Scores: A Narrative and Meta-Analytic Review," *Review of Educational Research*, Vol. 66, No. 3, 1996, pp. 227–268.

Cooper, Harris, Kelly Charlton, Jeff C. Valentine, Laura Muhlenbruck, and Geoffrey D. Borman, *Making the Most of Summer School: A Meta-Analytic and Narrative Review*, Vol. 65, Monographs of the Society for Research in Child Development, Malden, Mass.: Blackwell Publishers, 2000.

Cutting, Laurie E., and Hollis S. Scarborough, "Prediction of Reading Comprehension: Relative Contributions of Word Recognition, Language Proficiency, and Other Cognitive Skills Can Depend on How Comprehension Is Measured," *Scientific Studies of Reading*, Vol. 10, No. 3, 2006, pp. 277–299.

Jacob, Brian A., and Lars Lefgren, "Remedial Education and Student Achievement: A Regression-Discontinuity Design," *Review of Economics and Statistics*, Vol. 86, No. 1, 2004, pp. 226–244.

Keenan, Janice M., Rebecca S. Betjemann, and Richard K. Olson, "Reading Comprehension Tests Vary in the Skills They Assess: Differential Dependence on Decoding and Oral Comprehension," *Scientific Studies of Reading*, Vol. 12, No. 3, 2008, pp. 281–300.

Kim, James S., "Effects of a Voluntary Summer Reading Intervention on Reading Achievement: Results from a Randomized Field Trial," *Educational Evaluation and Policy Analysis*, Vol. 2006, No. 28, 2006, p. 235.

Kim, James S., and Jonathan Guryan, "The Efficacy of a Voluntary Summer Book Reading Intervention for Low-Income Latino Children from Language Minority Families," *Journal of Educational Psychology*, Vol. 102, No. 1, 2010, pp. 20–31.

Kim, James S., and David M. Quinn, "The Effects of Summer Reading on Low-Income Children's Literacy Achievement from Kindergarten to Grade 8: A Meta-Analysis of Classroom and Home Interventions," *Review of Educational Research*, Vol. 83, No. 3, 2013, pp. 386–431.

Kim, James S., and Thomas G. White, "Scaffolding Voluntary Summer Reading for Children in Grades 3 to 5: An Experimental Study," *Scientific Studies of Reading*, Vol. 12, No. 1, 2008, pp. 1–23.

Kim, Jimmy, "Summer Reading and the Ethnic Achievement Gap," *Journal of Education for Students Placed at Risk* (JESPAR), Vol. 9, No. 2, April 2004, pp. 169–188.

LeBuffe, Paul, Valerie Shapiro, and Jack Naglieri, *Devereux Student Strengths Assessment (DESSA)*, Villanova, Pa.: Devereux Center for Resilient Children, 2009.

Lipsey, Mark W., Kelly Puzio, Cathy Yun, Michael A. Hebert, Kasia Steinka-Fry, Mikel W. Cole, Megan Roberts, Karen S. Anthony, and Matthew D. Busick, *Translating the Statistical Representation of the Effects of Education Interventions into More Readily Interpretable Forms*, Washington, D.C.: National Center for Special Education Research, Institute of Education Sciences, U.S. Department of Education, NCSER 2013-3000, 2012.

Lockwood, J. R., Michael J. Weiss, and Daniel F. McCaffrey, "Estimating the Standard Error of the Impact Estimate in Individually Randomized Trials, with Clustering," paper presented at the Society for Research on Educational Effectiveness (SREE) Fall 2013 Conference, *Interdisciplinary Synthesis in Advancing Education Science*, Washington, D.C., September 26–28, 2013.

Mariano, Louis T., and Paco Martorell, "The Academic Effects of Summer Instruction and Retention in New York City," *Educational Evaluation and Policy Analysis*, Vol. 35, No. 1, 2013, pp. 96–117.

Matsudaira, Jordan D., "Mandatory Summer School and Student Achievement," *Journal of Econometrics*, Vol. 142, No. 2, 2008, pp. 829–850.

McCaffrey, Daniel F., Bing Han, and J. R. Lockwood, "Using Auxiliary Teacher Data to Improve Value-Added: An Application of Small Area Estimation to Middle School Mathematics Teachers," in Robert W. Lissitz and Hong Jiao, eds., *Value Added Modeling and Growth Modeling with Particular Application to Teacher and School Effectiveness*, Charlotte, N.C.: Information Age Publishing, 2013.

McCombs, Jennifer Sloan, Sheila Nataraj Kirby, and Louis T. Mariano, *Ending Social Promotion Without Leaving Children Behind: The Case of New York City*, Santa Monica, Calif.: RAND Corporation, MG-894-NYCDOE, 2009. As of August 24, 2010:
http://www.rand.org/pubs/monographs/MG894/

McCombs, Jennifer Sloan, Catherine H. Augustine, Heather Schwartz, Susan J. Bodilly, Brian McInnis, Dahlia S. Lichter, and Amanda Cross, *Making Summer Count: How Summer Programs Can Boost Children's Learning*, Santa Monica, Calif.: RAND Corporation, MG-1120-WF, 2011. As of November 12, 2014:
http://www.rand.org/pubs/monographs/MG1120.html

McCombs, Jennifer Sloan, John F. Pane, Catherine H. Augustine, Heather Schwartz, Paco Martorell, and Laura Zakaras, *Ready for Fall? Near-Term Effects of Voluntary Summer Learning Programs on Low-Income Students' Learning Opportunities and Outcomes—Appendix*, Santa Monica, Calif.: RAND Corporation, RR-815-WF, 2014. As of October 29, 2014:
http://www.rand.org/pubs/research_reports/RR815.html

Morsy, Leila, Michael Kieffer, and Catherine Snow, *Measure for Measure: A Critical Consumers' Guide to Reading Comprehension Assessments for Adolescents*, New York: Carnegie Corporation of New York, 2010.

Pendry, Patricia, and Stephanie Roeter, "Experimental Trial Demonstrates Positive Effects of Equine Facilitated Learning on Child Social Competence," *Human-Animal Interaction*, Vol. 1, No. 1, 2013. As of November 12, 2014:
http://ant2.homestead.com/pages/HAIB_Pendry__Roeter_2013.pdf

Pendry, Patricia, Alexa M. Carr, Annelise N. Smith, and Stephanie M. Roeter, "Improving Adolescent Social Competence and Behavior: A Randomized Trial of an 11-Week Equine Facilitated Learning Prevention Program," *Journal of Primary Prevention*, Vol. 35, No. 4, 2014, pp. 281–293.

Reardon, Sean F., "The Widening Academic Achievement Gap Between the Rich and the Poor: New Evidence and Possible Explanations," in Greg J. Duncan and Richard J. Murnane, eds., *Whither Opportunity? Rising Inequality, Schools, and Children's Life Chances,* New York: Russell Sage Foundation, 2011, pp. 1033–1681.

Schacter, John, and Booil Jo, "Learning When School Is Not in Session: A Reading Summer Day-Camp Intervention to Improve the Achievement of Exiting First-Grade Students Who Are Economically Disadvantaged," *Journal of Research in Reading*, Vol. 28, No. 2, 2005, pp. 158–169.

Schochet, Peter Z., *Technical Methods Report: Guidelines for Multiple Testing in Impact Evaluations*, Washington, D.C.: National Center for Education Evaluation and Regional Assistance, Institute of Education Sciences, U.S. Department of Education, NCEE 2008-4018, 2008.

U.S. Department of Education, *The Nation's Report Card*, web page, 2014. As of August 28, 2014:
http://nationsreportcard.gov

Wanzek, Jeanne, and Sharon Vaughn, "Research-Based Implications from Extensive Early Reading Interventions," *School Psychology Review*, Vol. 36, 2007, pp. 541–561.

Wanzek, Jeanne, Sharon Vaughn, Nancy K. Scammacca, Kristina Metz, Christy S. Murray, and Greg Roberts, "Extensive Reading Interventions for Students with Reading Difficulties After Grade 3," *Review of Educational Research*, Vol. 83, No. 2, 2013, pp. 163–195.

Wilkins, Chuck, Russell Gersten, Lauren Decker, Leslie Grunden, Sarah Brasiel, Kim Brunert, and Madhavi Jayanthi, *Does a Summer Reading Program Based on Lexiles Affect Reading Comprehension?* NCEE 2012-4006, Washington, D.C.: National Center for Education Evaluation and Regional Assistance, Institute of Education Sciences, U.S. Department of Education, 2012.

White, Thomas G., James S. Kim, Helen C. Kingston, and Lisa Foster, "Replicating the Effects of a Teacher-Scaffolded Voluntary Summer Reading Program: The Role of Poverty," *Reading Research Quarterly*, Vol. 49, No. 1, 2013, pp. 5–30.